A PLUME BOOK

MIND MAPS® AT WORK

TONY BUZAN, the leading authority on the brain and learning techniques, is the chairman of the Brain Foundation. He is the author of *The Mind Map® Book*, *Use Both Sides of Your Brain*, *Use Your Perfect Memory*, and *Speed Reading* (all available from Plume). He lectures all over the world and is published in one hundred countries and thirty languages. He advises multinational companies (among them HSBC, Oracle, Barclays International, and Hewlett-Packard), governments, leading businesses, educational authorities, and international Olympic athletes.

Praise for Tony Buzan

"This idea-rich, relentlessly upbeat manual proffers graphic images as an aid to unlock creative thinking or clarify emotions . . . Will challenge and stimulate the open-minded."
—*Publishers Weekly*

"If I am concerned about having too much to say or what to cover in a speech, I organize it by Mind Mapping the material."
—Kenneth Blanchard, author of *The One Minute Manager*

"Tony Buzan's *The Mind Map Book* will do for the brain what Stephen Hawking's *A Brief History of Time* did for the universe."
—Raymond Keene, O.B.E. Chess Grandmaster, and Mind Sports Correspondent, *The Times* (London)

"We teach—and use—Tony Buzan's techniques at EDS. *The Mind Map Book* is a valuable addition to our toolkit."
—Les Alberthal, chairman, president, and CEO, Electronic Data Systems

"The use of Mind Mapping is an integral part of my quality improvement program here at Boeing. This program has provided savings of over $10 million this year for my organization (ten times our goal)."
—Dr. Mike Stanley, Director of Special Projects, Boeing

"By exploiting the mind's associative power, it fixes memories and stirs your creative imagination."
—*Success*

ALSO BY TONY BUZAN

The Mind Map® Book
Speed Reading
Use Both Sides of Your Brain
Use Your Perfect Memory

Mind Maps at Work

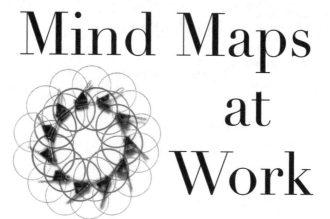

HOW TO BE THE BEST AT YOUR JOB AND STILL HAVE TIME TO PLAY

TONY BUZAN

A PLUME BOOK

PLUME
Published by Penguin Group
Penguin Group (USA) Inc., 375 Hudson Street, New York, New York 10014, U.S.A.
Penguin Group (Canada), 90 Eglinton Avenue East, Suite 700, Toronto, Ontario, Canada M4P 2Y3
(a division of Pearson Penguin Canada Inc.)
Penguin Books Ltd., 80 Strand, London WC2R 0RL, England
Penguin Ireland, 25 St. Stephen's Green, Dublin 2, Ireland (a division of Penguin Books Ltd.)
Penguin Group (Australia), 250 Camberwell Road, Camberwell, Victoria 3124, Australia
(a division of Pearson Australia Group Pty. Ltd.)
Penguin Books India Pvt. Ltd., 11 Community Centre, Panchsheel Park, New Delhi – 110 017, India
Penguin Books (NZ), cnr Airborne and Rosedale Roads, Albany, Auckland 1310, New Zealand
(a division of Pearson New Zealand Ltd.)
Penguin Books (South Africa) (Pty.) Ltd., 24 Sturdee Avenue, Rosebank,
Johannesburg 2196, South Africa

Penguin Books Ltd., Registered Offices: 80 Strand, London WC2R 0RL, England

Published by Plume, a member of Penguin Group (USA) Inc. This is an authorized reprint of a hard-
cover edition published by Thorsons.

First American Printing, December 2005
10 9 8 7 6 5 4 3 2 1

 REGISTERED TRADEMARK—MARCA REGISTRADA

LIBRARY OF CONGRESS CATALOGING-IN-PUBLICATION DATA

Buzan, Tony.
    Mind maps at work : how to be the best at your job and still have time to play / Tony Buzan.
        p. cm.
    Includes index.
    ISBN 0-452-28682-4
    1. Success in business—Handbooks, manuals, etc. 2. Job satisfaction—Handbooks, manuals, etc.
I. Title.

HF5386.B954 2005
650.1—dc22

                                                                    2005050953

Printed in the United States of America

CONTENTS

LIST OF MIND MAPS

ACKNOWLEDGEMENTS

With special thanks to my wonderful support team at Thorsons: Carole Tonkinson, Editorial Director; Susanna Abbott, Senior Commissioning Editor; Paul Effeny, Designer; Sonia Dobie, Cover Art Design Manager; Nicole Linhardt, Senior Production Controller; Liz Dawson, Publicity Manager; Laura Scaramella, Foreign Rights Director; and Belinda Budge, Managing Director.

A big thank you also to: Lucy Aitken for her dedication in helping me write this book; Matthew Cory for his superb edit; Stephanie Strickland for her fantastic illustrations; and Caroline Shott, my incredible literary manager, whose energy and dedication constantly amaze me.

Finally, a special thank you to my home team: Lesley Bias for her 'flying fingers'; Vanda North for her tireless work promoting Mind Maps around the world; my brother, Professor Barry Buzan, for his decades-long support of me and the Mind Mapping concept; and to my mother, Jean Buzan, who has always encouraged me to pursue my vision for Mind Maps.

TO MY READERS

This book is dedicated to everyone in the world's workplaces, whether you are a chief executive in China, an accountant in the UK or a nanny in Norway.

It is a response to the ever-expanding chorus of people who, over the years, have asked me for advice on how to apply Mind Maps to specific working situations.

On a practical level, Mind Maps can help you manage your workload, plan presentations and solve the toughest of business dilemmas. They can also fulfil the role of a life coach by helping you figure out what you want from your working life, while giving you a clear overview of complex situations and taking the stress from demanding obligations.

The more I have worked with different people in diverse organizations, the more roles I have noticed for Mind Maps in the workplace. As you will see from the examples throughout this book, Mind Maps are being used in astonishingly imaginative and creative ways in all kinds of enterprises, by all kinds of people all over the world.

On a personal level, Mind Maps have helped me appreciate that:

- The creativity of the human mind is infinite;
- Mind Maps are an expression of that infinite capacity;
- The infinite capacity of the human mind can create an infinite number of uses for Mind Maps.

This is why there is no limit to how Mind Maps help me and inspire me in the work I do—and why I want to share them with you.

Whatever kind of work you do and whatever role you perform, Mind Maps at Work will help you unleash your limitless creative potential. This will enrich your life and bring you success and satisfaction both at work and at home.

INTRODUCTION

Do you want to:

- Set goals and achieve them?
- Be more efficient at your job?
- Come up with ideas and creative solutions?
- Change career or start up your own business?
- Deliver excellent presentations with confidence?
- Stand up for yourself and your ideas?
- Be a key player at work?
- Lead your team to excellence?

If your answer is 'yes' to any of these questions this book is for you. *Mind Maps at Work* will help you set and achieve all your goals and ambitions in the workplace—and free up more time outside of it. With Mind Maps, your potential to impress your colleagues is infinite: Mind Maps are *the* tool for bringing out your talents and will help you make any challenge that comes your way an opportunity to demonstrate your brilliance.

Mind Maps will help you:

- Plan to perfection;
- Awaken your creative genius;
- Find inspired solutions to any problem;

- Recall facts under pressure;
- Motivate your team to success;
- Deliver lively and succinct presentations;
- Achieve a good work–life balance
- Love your work.

Mind Maps will enable you not only to survive, but to thrive positively at work—seeing beyond the fog of mundane details to a shining vision of where you and your business are heading. With this clearly in mind, you can calmly plot your course, confident in your ability to reach your goal.

Mind Maps have helped all kinds of individuals and businesses to achieve their potential and become great places to work. Mind Maps have also assisted millions of individuals all over the world to realize their dreams and achieve their ambitions. You will read about some of these success stories throughout the book, for example:

* **Planning perfection:** Con Edison, supplier of energy to New York, used Mind Maps to plan the restoration of power to Manhattan after 9/11;

* **Creative inspiration:** Design engineers at Boeing use Mind Maps in group meetings to brainstorm ideas;

* **Thinking big:** Mind Maps have been used to plan entire cities in the Gulf;

* **Success after disaster:** When Veritas in Singapore burnt down, the vice-president and his colleagues used Mind Maps to get it up and running again within 10 days;

* **Global rebranding:** John Scully, the man credited with taking Apple computers into the big league, used Mind Maps to develop his ideas and record his research for their new look;

✳ **Profit turnaround:** Mex, a restaurant chain in the USA, was brought back from the verge of bankruptcy with Mind Maps.

When you start using Mind Maps at work, you will be astounded by how much simpler and easier things become. Mind Maps are positive catalysts for change, clearing away confusion, illuminating targets and goals and—crucially—promoting the acquisition of knowledge.

Mind Maps can help you at work in an infinite number of ways because, like you, Mind Maps are workers. When Mind Maps are at work, they work hard, enabling you to think radiantly and unleash your own incredible potential. Mind Maps are also team players and are invaluable in facilitating communication:

- Between individuals;
- In the boardroom;
- Across whole companies.

Mind Maps can make being part of the team *enjoyable and creatively inspiring*. And as a team leader, your skills as a manager and motivator will be enhanced no end.

With Mind Maps on your side, you are able to achieve a much finer sense of work–life balance. And, for those of you who work at home, you can separate your home life and work commitments and have the best of both worlds.

Mind Maps will become your allies: they will be there to support you in any working situation.

By the time you have finished reading *Mind Maps at Work*, you will have gathered around you a potentially infinite team of Mind Map 'colleagues'. With the Mind Map manager, director, colleague, supporter and leader by your side, the possibilities are limitless . . .

Let *Mind Maps at Work* help *you* do the work.

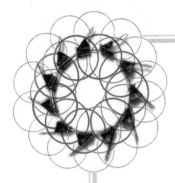

1

Unleash Your Infinite Creativity

Your brain is your key to success at work and the more effectively you use it, the more successful you will be. Just as you manage your workload and your team, you also need to manage your mind. If you stimulate it with the correct thinking and learning tools it will reward you with brilliant solutions to any kind of problem you might encounter. In short, you will be able to unleash your infinite, dazzling creativity.

TAPPING YOUR FULL POTENTIAL

As any successful businessperson will tell you, creativity and the ability to come up with new ideas are paramount to personal and organizational success, and every self-aware business in the world is seeking people who can contribute in this way. As Tuen Anders, Managing Partner of Enterprise IG in Amsterdam, comments:

> *'You can have the best factories in the world and the best products, but if you haven't got an idea, you're stuffed.'*

If creativity is so essential to being the best at work, why is it that people all over the world complain that their minds go blank when they are asked to come up with an original idea or an innovative answer? The simple explanation is that they are not engaging the full power of their brains. Typically, the average person only uses less than 1% of their brain in the areas of creativity, memory and learning—just think what could be achieved if we all used 20%, 40% or even 100%? Using Mind Maps, it is possible to begin to tap into our brain's full potential.

WHAT IS A MIND MAP?

A Mind Map is a colourful, visual form of note-taking that can be worked on by one person or a team of people. At its heart is a central idea or image. This is then explored by means of branches representing main ideas, which all connect to this central idea (see the 'Key Skills' Mind Maps, pp. 12 and 13).

From every 'main idea' branch there are 'sub-idea' branches which explore themes in greater depth. And to these branches of sub-ideas you can add more sub-branches, going on to explore the idea in even greater depth. Just as the branches are all connected, so are all the ideas in relation to each other, and this gives Mind Maps a depth and breadth of scope that a simple list of ideas cannot.

By working from the centre outwards, a Mind Map encourages your thoughts to behave in the same way. Soon your ideas will expand and you will *radiate creative thinking*—you will be an inspiration to yourself and others around you, and your imagination will know no bounds.

Once you have experienced how liberating a feeling this can be, you will discover there is no limit to how much Mind Maps can help you at work. You can use a Mind Map to explore any idea, concept or problem, from planning a report, a presentation or a business strategy to working out what kind of career you want to pursue. On a personal level, you can use them to plan your day ahead, the coming week, month or year and, indeed, your *life*. At work, Mind Maps can help you to excel in any area that demands clarity and creativity.

How do Mind Maps work?

How many times have you been at work and written a list of things you need to do on a piece of blank white paper with a blue or black pen? You started at the top and worked down, and as you completed items on the list you ticked off things or drew a line through them as you went along. But didn't it annoy you that you never seemed to get to the end of the list? Instead, you probably made a new list incorporating some of the elements of the old list. When this has gone on for some time, it can feel as if the lists are controlling you rather than vice versa.

Because lines, sequences, letters, numbers and lists are all mental skills of the left brain, using just these when you are brainstorming will be creatively restricting as they only engage the left side of your brain. This is the side of the brain that traditionally has been associated with good business sense. However, to truly be creative you also need to use your imagination, which is the realm of the right brain. Right-brain mental skills include interpreting colour, image, rhythm and spatial awareness.

Mind Maps use letters and numbers and they *also* use colour and image, which means that they engage the left *and* the right sides of brain. This is why you can increase your thinking power synergetically when you use Mind Maps. Each side of the brain simultaneously feeds off *and* strengthens the other in a manner which provides limitless creative potential.

Don't take sides

Research by Professor Sperry in the 1970s showed that everybody has full left- and right-brain potential. It is not limited to men being better at left-brain activities and women being stronger at right-brain activities, which was the long-held assumption. People have an extensive range of intellectual and creative skills that they only partly use. What is more, if both the left and right brain are used, both sides become stronger, engaging with each other to bolster their combined creative output. This, in turn, strengthens the ability for greater association. This means that your creative and intellectual firepower has the potential to increase even more.

The greatest minds

The education systems in many of the world's developed economies force students into choosing, at quite an early age, whether their core subjects will be 'scientific' or 'artistic'. Yet if you look at the world's greatest examples of creative genius, you will notice that great artists are often great scientists and vice versa. Leonardo da Vinci had a scientific approach towards creating some of the world's finest art. And Nobel Prize winners have frequently straddled both 'scientific' and 'artistic' theory. Geniuses work hard both their left and right brains, and are constantly searching for new experiences and new solutions with their marvellous minds.

YOUR PERSONAL SEARCH ENGINE

Your brain is a multiplier and multiplies ideas by association. Mind Maps work on two key principles—imagination and association. Your brain searches for connections in a similar way to a search engine on the Internet when you type in a word. The next time you are logged on to a search engine, type in 'Mind Maps' and look at the astonishing number of references on the Internet—the last count nudged 6,000,000 at time of going to press. Think about your brain in the same way as that search engine, but with the added knowledge that it is infinitely more powerful.

Mind Maps are such an effective thinking tool because they work *with* your brain and encourage it to develop associations between ideas: each branch you add to your Mind Map is associated with the previous branch. They are a visual manifestation of how your brain thinks. This is why Mind Maps rewrite the rules. They constantly draw your attention to what is at the heart of the matter and, by association and imagination, lead you to significant conclusions. Like a street map, Mind Maps will show you obvious signs about how to get to your destination. They will help you unleash the creative genius within and make you and your powerful brain even more essential to your employer.

Start with yourself

It's time for you to tap into this more natural and stimulating way to use your brain. Try drawing a Mind Map now. You will need the following:

- A blank piece of paper;
- Coloured pens, pencils or crayons;
- Your imagination.

Rather than think about your job, think about yourself. What are you good at? What are your particular skills?

MAKING YOUR FIRST MIND MAP—KEY SKILLS

1. Take a blank piece of paper and turn it on its side. This will give your Mind Map the room it needs to expand in all directions.

2. Draw an image in the centre of the page to represent your main idea—in this instance, your personal skills. You might want to draw a picture of yourself or, for example, if you are a doctor, an image of a stethoscope. Write your name or your profession, job title or, simply, 'my skills' above, below or inside it. Use colours all the time when you are Mind Mapping. This will make the process more fun for you and more interesting and memorable for your brain.

3. Choose a colour and draw a curved branch from your central image. Write down a word that relates to an area of your skills. For instance, if you have good communication skills, make a branch labelled 'communicator'. You will need a branch for 'knowledge', which you will later be able to expand on. Next, label branches 'experience' and 'goals'. Lastly, consider what other particular attributes you possess which are not covered by these categories. In the example below, there is a branch labelled 'independent' as this can be an important quality for leaders and self-starters.

4. Only use one word per branch, because a single word is better at triggering thoughts than phrases or sentences. Ensure that the branch is touching the central image. If the branches are connected on the page, the ideas they hold will also connect in your head.

5. Draw sub-branches from your main branch, using words to develop the theme. For example, if you think you are good at organizing, a Mind Map can take that further. What is it you are good at organizing and how do you go about achieving your results?

6. Draw pictures throughout when creating your Mind Map—the images will assist and prompt your imagination. They don't have to be works of art—rough sketches are fine. The important thing is for the image to prompt your memory.

You will notice how drawing a Mind Map of your skills is a different process to writing up your CV, where your hobbies and interests are tagged on to the end. The Mind Map gives a much truer and more rounded picture of you as a person, and demonstrates *all* you have to offer and where you want to go.

A Mind Map explores every potential avenue that is open to you. Enough people have made a living out of something they feel passionate about—and so can you. If you would like further inspiration for your Mind Map, take a look at the colour Skills Mind Map. Here, the main branches leading from the centre are 'experience', 'knowledge', 'communicator', 'independent' and 'goals'. Each of these themes is developed in turn with words and pictures. For instance, if you follow the sub-branches from the main 'goals' branch, you will see an interest in 'energy' is indicated, which is then more narrowly defined by the word 'renewable'; from here three branches break out—'research', 'wind' and 'water': next to 'wind' is a drawing of a wind turbine and next to 'research' is a microscope. The overall result of this is a vivid and lasting mental representation of a career goal.

The sky's the limit

Although what you Mind Map and the images and words you add to it are entirely up to you, you do need to follow the Mind Map guidelines above to draw and develop your Mind Maps. This is not to restrict your freedom in any way; on the contrary, it *gives you* infinite intellectual freedom. This is because these guidelines work closely with how your brain functions—by imagination and association. Just as our bodies are all fundamentally similar, but at the same time uniquely and subtly different in expression, so it is with Mind Maps. If your Mind Map keeps developing and 'outgrows' your single sheet of paper, then carry on. Stick together as many sheets as you need and make it as large as you like.

CREATIVITY AND IDEAS

According to the global branding and design experts at Enterprise IG, many companies and their employees are on a creativity treadmill. As the company's report, 'Winning in an Information Age', points out:

To inspire and grow, you have to create. You need the helping hand of imagination. Creativity. Yet many businesses have lost the spark of innovation and creativity. What was new and exciting yesterday quickly becomes ho-hum today. Coming up with one great creative idea isn't good enough any more. It's the ability to generate an endless stream of new ideas that matters.'

MIND MAPS — YOUR IDEAS MACHINE

Minds Maps can help you think creatively about anything, and thinking creatively is the way to achieve what you want. In the workplace this might be to make your team the best in your department. Mind Maps will help you to assess and reshape your team goals and then match the key strengths of your team members to these goals. On a more personal level, you can use Mind Maps creatively to work out how you want to develop your career and to decide what your next career move should be.

Your brilliant brain

Nowadays many of us wonder how we would manage without personal computers, and are amazed at their speed and the many different functions they can perform. In fact, just one of your brain cells has more power than that computer and you have a million million brain cells. Just think of all that power that is lying dormant in your head. With that potential on your side, you could easily launch your own company, come up with a creative idea that challenges an existing status quo, or make shrewd investments.

Mind Maps can help you to achieve ambitions you had previously written off as too far-fetched. For example, imagine you always wanted to write a detective story. You have a vague idea of what the plot might be but have never got your project off the ground. When you Mind Map the plot you will be able to develop your idea to the point where you can actually begin writing—you can make your dream a reality. Start your Mind Map by drawing an image in the centre of the page, for example the murder weapon, the motive for the crime or the central character. Your main ideas branches could include the basic plot, the characters in it, how their lives are interlinked, the motive for the crime and so on. Like a certain detective's 'little grey cells', your Mind Map can analyze each aspect of the plot and characterization forensically. In this way, you could map out the scene of the crime, using 'sense' branches such as 'sight', 'sound' and 'smell' to search for potential clues. Similarly, you might use your Mind Map to role play your characters, investigating, branch by branch, their appearance background and history. And when you begin to draw links between your characters, and between them and the crime, the creative power of Mind Maps is displayed as the complex plot is revealed in front of you.

In addition, you could use your Mind Map to work out when you will make time to write it, where you will send it for possible publication and who you could ask for advice and input. When you have Mind Mapped it, your novel will be less of a distant dream and more of a reality.

Mind Map liberation

Mind Maps will liberate you from your mental rut in the workplace and will:

- help you solve problems;
- save you time;
- help you to be more creative;
- clarify a situation;
- help you to plan;
- help you to communicate;

- give you perspective on a situation;
- help you to remember;
- help you to organize.

This will mean that you will:

- feel intellectually and creatively liberated at work;
- enjoy your work;
- recognize that you are an 'ideas machine'.

MANAGING YOUR TEAM POTENTIAL

In many workplaces, the potential for a more creative approach is ignored. Creativity can be one of those vital talents that is overlooked in favour of more traditional business or academic skills. If you are a manager, whether of a small team or a large division, there are countless ways in which a more creative approach can make for a happier workforce and a more congenial atmosphere at work. Examples of this might include:

✳ If you and your team have been asked to come up with a new strategy for a key client, set up a meeting and ask everybody to Mind Map their ideas for a new strategy in advance. When you get together you can compare and discuss your Mind Maps. You will be amazed at how many innovative ideas you will come up with between you. In addition, your team will have a greater sense of ownership of the business plan you eventually implement.

✳ If a staff room needs decorating, make it a team effort. Encourage everybody to debate their ideas by using Mind Maps. They will enjoy being there much more if they have had a say in what it looks like.

❋ Ask team members for their suggestions for any staff parties and again use Mind Maps to discuss all the available options.

❋ Organize a team day or evening that will captivate everybody's interests. Mind Map all the interests of the people on your team, from darts to dancing, and invite them to share their expertise. You will be surprised to see your colleagues in a completely new light.

NEXT STEPS

Make sure that you give your brain as much opportunity as possible to be creative. Keep exposing yourself to new experiences and new people, and try to activate all of your senses as often as possible. The more ideas you have, the more possible associations you have to make. Since you never know what experience or idea might come in useful, you should embrace each moment of the day.

To remind yourself, draw a Mind Map of how you can encourage your brain to make every day a more creative experience.

Ways to unleash your creativity

Whenever you need to think creatively or radiantly at work, always think of Mind Maps first. Use them to explore ideas and help you think 'out of the box'. To optimize the creative potential of your Mind Maps, it is essential to keep your mind 'fit' and to maintain and increase your mind's database of ideas and knowledge. The more facts you have at your disposal, the more the potential creative outcomes there will be.

- **Listen and learn**—Listen to yourself. If you have a tendency to interrupt other people when they are speaking to you, consider how you feel when someone interrupts you.

A person who is loud and talks over other people does not come across as a sympathetic member of a work team. If you take the time to listen to others, not only will you learn much more, but you will also find a willing ear when you need somebody to listen to you.

When you realize how much you can learn by listening more, your thirst for learning will be re-awakened. This may give you the impetus to take a distance-learning or evening class. For example, you could learn how to speak a foreign language, master a specific computer software package or take up graphic design. Even if the subject matter is not immediately work-related, your new breadth of experience will add to your creative potential.

- **Read**—Reading books that you would not normally select can be immensely satisfying for your brain. Think radically next time you are choosing a book. If it is not one you would read as a rule, there is even more reason to give it a try. And if you read the same newspaper on the train to work every morning, buy an alternative. You never know, you might just prefer it, and even if you don't you will have accumulated a new experience and perspective on life. When you read something you want to remember, make a point of Mind Mapping it. Books can be Mind Mapped with the title as the central idea, the chapters as the main branches and the themes and your impressions as sub-branches.

- **Doodle and draw**—Even if you consider yourself not to be artistic, the doodles on your notepad show that there is an artist inside you, desperate to break free and reveal your hidden talents. While you may not be about to win a major art prize, if you give free rein to your artistic urges, you may be surprised what you achieve. By unleashing your imagination with doodles or drawings on your Mind Maps, you will help the process of making creative connections— and solutions.

- **Broaden your horizons**—Seize every opportunity to make new friends and contacts, in business and your personal life. They will give you a fresh perspective on life that is vital in terms of keeping your creativity sharpened and your imagination awakened. And they might come in useful one day in a business capacity. Travel broadens the mind as well as your frame of reference so you are not limited to the same experiences as everyone else in your office: you have been bold and tried something different. If you always go on holiday to the beach in the summer, try something completely different instead, such as skiing or snow-boarding in the winter.

- **Dream and daydream**—If you can remember your dreams on waking up, write them down immediately. Keep pen and paper ready by your bed for this purpose. Yours dreams could hold some interesting insights into your life, personality and relationships. In a similar way, daydreaming is a vital way of engaging with right-brain activity and is good exercise for your imagination. Mind Maps are the perfect tool for developing your daydreams.

- **Keep your Mind Map machine fit**—Your brain is as much an organ of your body as your heart and lungs. There is good reason for the Latin saying, *mens sana in corpore sano*—a healthy mind in a healthy body. Not only do your brain cells need a plentiful supply of oxygen and nutrients to nourish them, they also need to operate *synergetically* in a healthy body. (For more on this, see my books *Headstrong* and *The Power of Physical Intelligence*.) This is why exercise is vitally important for a vibrant mind.

Fight the impulse when returning home from work to collapse in a heap in front of the TV. Instead, join a gym or find a keep-fit class in your area. Go with a friend so you can motivate each other. Gym membership rockets in January as everyone fights the post-celebratory bulge, but come February, the motivation disappears and old habits return. If Oyou make exercise an enjoyable and fun part of your life, your brain will thank you for it.

Over the next few chapters, we will be looking at how to use Mind Maps to deal with specifics in the workplace, such as how to use them to run meetings like clockwork and deliver presentations effortlessly. You will be able to summon ideas into your brain—and remember them. Your brain—your creativity machine—is geared up and ready to go. To begin with, we will look at how to solve problems using Mind Maps.

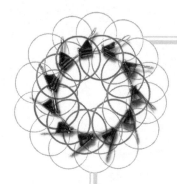

2

The Fresh
Approach
to Problem
Solving

One of the key skills required to be successful at work is the ability to find speedy and imaginative solutions to the challenges and difficulties that inevitably arise.

AVOIDING THE BRAIN STRAIN

When confronted with a problem that needs our attention, all too often we try to 'force' our brains into coming up with a solution. Not only is this a poor way to resource our creativity, this approach can result in stress which in turn becomes compounded when we lose sleep at night, tossing and turning as our minds wrestle with the problem. Straining your brain in this way when tired and overwrought will not result in a satisfactory solution.

Instead, it is far preferable to use Mind Maps whenever you are in a situation which demands clarity, diagnosis and a solution. View the situation as a positive challenge, an opportunity to demonstrate your skills and flex your creative muscles.

You can use Mind Mapping for solving problems in the workplace by taking one of two routes:

1. **Start with the problem** itself as your central image and work *forwards*. For instance, if you have been receiving complaints from

customers about poor standards of service, then your central image could be a frowning dissatisfied customer.

2.   **Start with a solution** as your central image and work *backwards*. Here, your grumpy dissatisfied customer transforms into a smiling satisfied customer who tells friends and family about your wonderful organization.

These two approaches are equally valid. In fact, it may bring the problem into clearer focus for you and your team if you draw both Mind Maps and notice where they overlap.

RISING TO THE CHALLENGE

Problems at work come in all shapes and sizes. They can vary in severity from a minor hiccup in an otherwise smooth-running operation, to a major problem that may threaten the existence of a business concern. Sometimes difficulties can appear as if out of the blue, while at other times they develop over an extended period of time. In either case, once the existence of a problem is identified, the moment has come to rise to the challenge and use Mind Maps to navigate your way to the optimum solution.

Coping with immediate problems

Imagine the scene. You are the manager at Books U Love, an independent bookshop. It is Christmas Eve and the shop is packed with last-minute shoppers. Tempers are frayed among the customers who want their shopping experience to be over as they have to rush home and wrap their presents. Meanwhile, the staff have been on their feet all day and are longing for the shop to close.

You are called over to a till where a customer is complaining. A book that she had reserved for her daughter weeks ago cannot be found and there are no more copies in store. The sales assistant is explaining that the books can only be held for a week and that she should have come in to pick it up sooner. The customer, not taking kindly to being told what she should have done, is becoming increasingly irate and has asked to speak to the manager.

While your instinct may be to groan and run away, this is your store and your role is to take responsibility for the situation. As the manager, you have to toe a careful line between the customer and the sales assistant. Steeling yourself, you take half a minute to draw a mental Mind Map in your head of the situation in hand. Your central image is one of a satisfied customer whose Christmas is definitely not going to be ruined by an errant book. The main branches of the Mind Map could be:

1. **Finding a solution**—you need to find a solution to the immediate problem of finding a book for the customer.

2. **The reputation of the shop**—you do not want potential customers discussing poor customer service at Books U Love over their turkey and sprouts.

3. **Your sales assistant**—there are only a few hours of the working day to go and this is the first Christmas she has worked in the shop. The frenetic pace has left her frazzled.

4. **The problem**—you need to analyze the problem, not only to come up with a solution but also to ensure that it doesn't happen again in the future.

5. **Yourself**—you do not want this experience to colour what has so far been a successful time managing the shop. You have to be supportive of both your staff and your customers.

You approach the potentially explosive situation calmly. Having worked out your Mind Map, you are in control of the situation. Here is how the Mind Map informs your action:

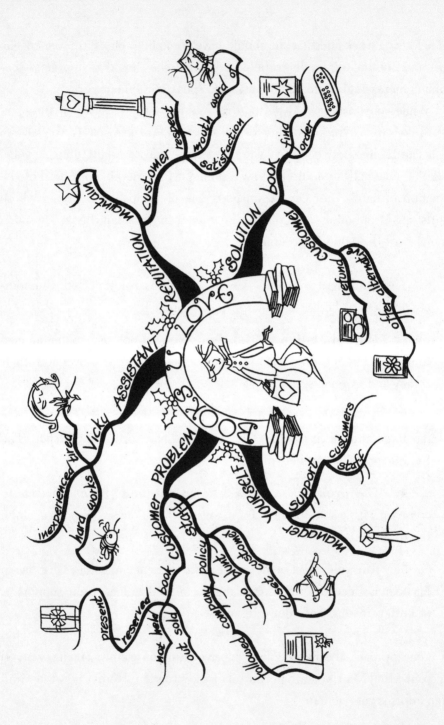

1. You ask the sales assistant if she would like to take her tea break now. You can tell she is upset and needs a break from being on the shop floor so she can calm down. She is likely to upset other customers or team members by taking out her frustration on them.

2. You listen to the customer's point of view. You take her to one side and ask her what the problem is. Rolling her eyes to heaven, she explains again, but now she becomes calmer. She appreciates that you are taking the time to understand the situation for yourself. While you secretly agree with your sales assistant—you think that the customer should have come in sooner to pick up the book—perhaps this wasn't explained to her properly when she ordered it. This may have been the fault of your staff. If this is the case, then you as the manager need to take responsibility.

3. Thinking of the shop's long-term reputation, you explain that ordered books are held in store only for one week and you apologize that this was not explained to her at the time. You tell her that you will do your best to locate another copy and that you will ring around your local contacts. If you are unable to find a copy, offer her an alternative book free of charge and give her a Books U Love book token to spend in the store after Christmas. Also offer to take the customer's order again and explain that the book will be in store in the first week of January should she wish to come in and pick it up. You apologize that this particular book will not arrive in time for her daughter to unwrap on Christmas Day, but say that you hope her daughter enjoys the book you recommended as it is very popular and your own daughter loves it. The customer is now smiling as she accepts the token. She leaves the shop and will now tell her friends and family about how well you treated her. This is good news for you and your shop. If it had been bad news, word would have travelled like wildfire, fuelled by the customer's anger and frustration.

4. You then talk to the sales assistant and explain that as neither of you took the order, you can't be sure of what the customer was and wasn't told. You make a mental note to make sure that all your staff are aware of how to take orders. This is something you can look at in the New Year. By now, the sales assistant has calmed down and accepts what you say. You have dealt with a difficult situation between the customer and the sales assistant in a calm and peaceful way.

Problem solved.

This example shows how indispensable Mind Maps can be as your *first port of call* when you are faced with a problem at work. Even if you don't have coloured pens and paper to hand, your brain can still conjure up a mental Mind Map, a virtual picture of the situation to help you work out a plan of action.

The Mind Map gives you control over all the information relating to the problem, in a secure and stable framework, showing you the 'big picture' as well as the details, so allowing you to address the problem in a comprehensive and integrated way. As Harry Scott of Speakers International says:

'The essence of Mind Mapping is that it is a totally natural process. A Mind Map puts everything into one single picture that tells the complete story.'

The importance of the central image of the Mind Map when you are creating a mental Mind Map is paramount, as it informs absolutely everything that you want to achieve, or the crux of the problem you need to solve.

Mind Mapping in action: Con Edison

After 9/11 and the collapse of the World Trade Center, all the vital utilities to large areas of the city were thrown into chaos.

The communication lines, gas, electricity, water and sewerage networks were in disarray. This haemorrhaging of the utilities presented a genuine threat to businesses and residents alike.

Con Edison, the supplier of gas and electricity to the residents of New York, faced the massive challenge of restoring power to the residents of Manhattan. However, the company had experience with one crucial tool—Mind Maps. Con Edison hosted teams from all regions of public utility to develop a complex action plan to route their way through the crisis. A mega-Mind Map was drawn up, on which all the problems and necessary solutions were laid out. Each step was prioritized and sequenced, and the impact of the failure of one utility on another examined, and this formed the basis of an operations guide. For instance, in some cases the re-establishment of electricity supplies was essential before the monitoring and recommencement of the movement of water, gas and sewerage.

Con Edison created a Mind Map in conjunction with a large-screen monitor to provide live-time data displays. The Mind Map included web-links to all key documents. In this way, information was easily disseminated among teams. Normal utilities' service was resumed efficiently and, by identifying and documenting the risks faced and the dangers involved, safely.

The coming together of the resources, ideas and know-how of the utilities through the medium of Mind Maps minimized the distress experienced by an already traumatized community.

Coping with long-term problems

When you get into the habit of Mind Mapping when faced with a problem, you will begin to notice recurring patterns. This may lead you to identify the need for change at your business or place of work (*see* Chapter 4).

Imagine you are the manager of a high-street bank, Smith & Son, that has been losing customers to competitor banks. You urgently need to identify the reasons why you are falling behind the competition. You can do this by drawing up a Mind Map to help you focus on where the problems lie and what you might be able to do to solve them.

Here is a basic guide to drawing your Mind Map:

1. Draw the Smith & Son's logo as the central image on your Mind Map. In this way, you are illustrating that you are committed to keeping the bank open by facing up to its problems.

2. Next, consider each of the problems faced by the bank in turn. This will include all the elements of the competition including online banking, other high-street banks and phone banking services. Each one of these topics will be condensed into the main branches: 'strengths', 'action', 'hours' and 'competition'.

3. Explore each of the elements along the main branches more thoroughly in the sub-branches. For instance, from the 'competition' branch you can explore with sub-branches the quality of service Smith & Son provide in relation to the competition, in terms of its speed, range of services and length of opening hours. Similarly, from the 'strengths' branch you can indicate the loyalty of customers and staff.

While there may be problems at the bank that have been brewing for a long time, it may be only when you start Mind Mapping that you appreciate the extent to which they are having a negative impact on your business.

Through your Mind Map, you can see that radical change is required. You need to take urgent action. (*See* colour Mind Map of Smith & Sons.)

At the same time, you can also take note of what the bank is doing well and make sure that you protect it. For example, years of tradition and good service are huge benefits which work in your favour. There is a balance here and Mind Mapping will help you to find it.

By involving your colleagues in this process and discussing the problems with them, you will have everyone on your side when it comes to implementing solutions. This is vital—you need to sell the solution to them, not just tell it to them. Here, the Mind Map will play a huge role in putting the bank's predicament into a wider context.

For instance, your staff may have to work longer hours on Saturdays. If you are working together on problem-solving with the Mind Map from the start, they will have a better understanding of why this is necessary. By the same token, it is possible that your colleagues can contribute new insights as to how a problem may be solved. Consultation and compromise are valuable tools in efficient and dynamic management.

MIND MAPS AND THE ART OF COMPROMISE

While effective problem-solving can involve compromise, for compromise to work it has to come about as the result of skilled and artful negotiation.

Walk it out to work it out

It will help if you can distance yourself from the problem in hand. Take a short walk and return to the problem, fresh and clear-headed.

The Romans coined the phrase *solvitas perambulum*, which translates as 'solve it as you walk'. They believed that

---

the combination of fresh air, removing themselves physically from the source of the problem, light physical exercise and creative inspiration from nature worked wonders if they needed to sort through an issue in their minds.

The state in which your imagination is able to run free is ideal for making associations on a Mind Map. By giving your brain a rest from repeatedly raking over every aspect of a problem, you will find you are much more likely to come up with a solution.

Effective negotiation with Mind Maps

Traditionally, negotiation has been seen in a 'them v us', 'unions v management' context. The participants enter a negotiation with their 'wish lists' and then become angry and frustrated when they don't manage to achieve everything on the list. If both sides enter the process of negotiation in this way, at best the resolution can only be partial, and neither side will be completely satisfied.

Preparing such a 'wish list' cuts off all avenues of creative thought. It is like having a number of roadblocks hindering the routes in and out of a city. A Mind Map, however, allows you to retain your goals while remaining sensitive to the bigger picture. At the same time, your views and those of others can be mapped and areas of overlap can be identified as the basis for negotiation.

A meeting of Mind Maps

The Gulf Finance House in Bahrain asked me if I would work with them on the development of major new projects, including the building from scratch of islands to house entire cities.

I was invited to Bahrain to see the company and to go over its strategic plan with them in order to assess whether I would be interested in working on the project. After three days of exchanging information, it came to the point of negotiation. Of course, the prime object of all negotiations is to reach a conclusion that is satisfactory conceptually to all parties and *beneficial,* over the short, medium and long term.

Traditional negotiation is incredibly long-winded and inefficient. This time I sat down with the managing director and I Mind Mapped what I wanted to do with them; meanwhile, he Mind Mapped what he wanted me to do with them. We agreed that we would start to negotiate only when we had decided exactly what we wanted from each other. After completing our Mind Maps, he then told me all the things he wanted. The extraordinary thing was that, when it was my turn to present what I wanted from our partnership, I had virtually nothing to say to him. Our Mind Maps were almost identical. Mind Maps made it very easy for both of us to negotiate because we realized that we both wanted the same thing.

Tips for successful negotiation

After both parties have presented the information on their respective Mind Maps, there will be a chance for discussion and debate. The following tips will complement your Mind Map to ensure that you get what you want out of the discussions:

1.   **Use silence as a positive space**—If there is a pause during negotiation, the onus is not on you to fill it. It might help to have a natural break at that point while your brains are working out what you really think. Silence can be a valuable tool—welcome it and use it.

2. **Listen properly**—Listen in a total way to the person with whom you are negotiating. This does not mean just going through the motions of listening so that you can respond with your thoughts at the end. If you listen properly to people, they will repay the favour. You will be able to understand more clearly where they stand in relation to the points that you have drawn up on your Mind Map. As a result, the negotiation will be more successful and you will both stand more chance of getting what you want.

Negotiating with Mind Maps

Kathleen Kelly Reardon is the author of *The Secret Handshake* and *The Skilled Negotiator*. She says:

'One of the things that comes to mind that I think is highly relevant to Mind Mapping is that the skilled negotiator thinks in terms of options. The less skilled negotiator thinks in terms of limitations. One of the kisses of death in negotiation is to be predictable. If you can use Mind Mapping, you can think in terms of multiple paths and that is one of the things I train people in all the time.'

The Mind Map is the only tool you need to work out what you want from any kind of negotiation. If a Mind Map is used by all parties around the negotiating table, then all parties stand to gain from employing Mind Maps for successful negotiation.

GETTING ADVICE AT WORK

We all need advice at work. Whether it is when dealing with a particular difficulty that you are encountering with your own job or, on a wider scale, seeing the way to formulating significant new company policy, you can only benefit from getting the views of others.

Clearly, where you go to first for advice will depend on the nature of the problem. In some cases, you might consider whether your partner or family know enough about what you do at work to be able to help.

Alternatively, you might feel able to confide in certain members of your team. Whomever you do turn to, the important thing is to ask for advice when you need it and then incorporate that advice onto a Mind Map. This will give you a much clearer picture of your particular situation and an insight into the best course of action.

For too long, there has been a myth in the workplace that if you need help, you cannot be doing your job properly. On the contrary, it is infinitely preferable to work as a team. By working creatively together synergetically, you will have at your disposal ideas and creativity larger than the sum of your team's individual contributions.

Creating a support system

Support systems, whether formal or informal, exist at work so that problems can be shared. If you are proactive and set up a support system, your workforce will become a happier team. Start by creating a Mind Map to form a support system:

MIND MAPPING A SUPPORT SYSTEM

1. As your central image, draw a smiling employee. This is an example of starting with the solution first and working backwards, where your goal is to achieve what is represented by that central image. Because your brain is not a 'problem solver', but a 'solution finder', it will work towards the vision that you give it. When you are Mind Mapping your support system, if you have a central image of a happy employee,

37

all your associations will automatically radiate out from that central idea/goal.

2. Draw curved branches from your central image with one word written along the branch and touching it. Each branch represents a way in which you can develop a support system at work. In larger companies, this could involve a centralized helpline or the confidential services of a counsellor. In any organization, one branch could represent a 'buddy system' where, on joining, employees are assigned another member of staff to help them with anything from how to work the photocopier to deep-seated concerns about their work, expressed in strictest confidence. You could include senior members of staff as well as any industry trade associations.

In certain situations, it is necessary to ensure confidentiality within a team, and in this context a Mind Map can be used as a 'secret code'. To accomplish this, you and the team members decide on the specific meanings and significance of certain colours, symbols and words, which only you and the team will know. For example, green in your Mind Map could always signify 'agreement'. In this way, a secondary layer of information, available only to those who hold the key, can be embedded within the Map.

3. Use sub-branches to extend your thinking on each suggestion on the main branches. Industry trade associations, for instance, frequently offer free legal advice or, at the very least, a telephone conversation with a lawyer who has years of experience in dealing with your industry's legal problems. Use colour here to clarify which suggestions you think are the most appropriate, practical and relevant to your particular workplace.

4. Use the Mind Map to bounce your ideas off other people in your team. Then listen to their ideas, incorporating them into your Mind Map.

5. Present your ideas as a team to your team leader using the Mind Map as your central focus. (*See* Chapter 7 for more ideas on using Mind Maps to help banish presentation nerves.)

MASTERMIND GROUPS

At times, it will be beneficial to marshal the widest possible help and advice to find the optimum solution to a problem. Imagine how it would be if you could consult with the finest brains the world has ever known. A Mastermind group can do just this. Using your imagination, you can discuss your problems with the likes of Leonardo da Vinci or Stephen Hawking. You might also want to mix outstanding creativity with modern business acumen. So alongside da Vinci or Hawking, you might consider juxtaposing the ideas of a modern business brain such as Martha Lane-Fox, co-creator of the web site lastminute.com, who made a cool £30 million in just a few years.

To compile your Mastermind group, think about who inspires you from the rich seam of talented people who have left a creative legacy. Perhaps there is a musician who has always been your hero, a singer whose lyrics have a particular poignancy for you, a writer whose opinions you respect or a top-rated chef who has always impressed you with his imaginative and unorthodox approach to food and drink.

The selection can be as varied as you want it to be and there are no rules or boundaries: they can be dead or alive, male or female, young or old. The only thing they must have in common is that they all inspire you.

When you have formed your Mastermind group, put your problem to them; listen to their lively debate about the best course of action for you. Your brain has a remarkable and hidden capability for 'separating itself out' into different personalities and then for seeing any situation from the perspective of each personality. Your Mastermind group gives your brain the structure with which to do this, and to do it from the perspectives of:

- Strength;
- Creativity;
- Originality;
- Power;

- Intelligence;
- Wisdom;
- Focus;
- Concern.

Using the full power of your imagination, address the group as if it were real, alternating between general discussions and one-on-one discussions in which you and your chosen Mastermind have in-depth conversations about the situation. You will be surprised how real your Masterminds become and how the advice they give will be radically different from anything you might have thought of in your customary way of thinking. As you go, make a Mind Map and add the advice that your Mastermind group has given you.

Alternatively, single out a particular hero or heroine from your Master-mind group and have a discussion with them about the problem. Think about what they would say and heed their advice.

As before, incorporate their advice into your Mind Map and see what actions this now indicates.

Great figures in history have all benefited from having inspirational people around them who guided, advised, motivated and, above all else, helped them when it came to problem solving.

Alexander the Great

King Philip of Macedonia invested hugely in bringing up his son, Alexander. He gave him free rein to choose his own learning, so Alexander opted for physical combat, culture and the arts, philosophy and science. In each area, he had the best tuition available in that field, being tutored, for example, by Aristotle in philosophy.

As a result of his rich and varied Mastermind group, Alexander the Great became a natural, visionary leader who established over 100 universities during his reign to improve and enhance the learning of his subjects.

The Mastermind group at work

Real visionaries understand that there will always be problems, particularly if the company is undergoing a period of change. Traditionally, too much emphasis has been placed on the manager–employee relationship. Instead, if teams are set up across different departments with the express intention of problem-solving, they can bring a much wider perspective to the task.

Mastermind groups can also help departments keep in touch with what they are doing, and enable individuals to acquaint themselves with what others in the company do. This can benefit the company's employees in terms of seeing the bigger picture and also help both management and employees to recognize where in the company particular talents will be of most use. To obtain the benefit of the teamed creative input of your Mastermind group, you need to Mind Map all the different perspectives and opinions to see how they fit together.

Mastermind groups in practice

If you are in management, try putting together a few Mastermind groups to meet at different times of the month. Every six months, shake up the groups so that everyone is introduced to new faces and ideas. This assists in getting everyone to work well together and will bring a reference point to team members which is outside their immediate scope. Ensure that when the Mastermind groups meet up, Mind Maps are used as a form of minute-taking and that they are shared between group members before each meeting (*see* p. 190).

MIND MAPS: TAKING OFF THE PRESSURE

As a brain-smart worker you will be aware that your brain does not come up with the best solutions when you are stressed, frustrated, overworked and rushing about trying to put out hundreds of little fires, all of which have the potential to become full-blown conflagrations.

You also know that making endless lists is an unenlightened approach to problem-solving. By using Mind Maps, your brain will provide you with elegant and powerful solutions when it is relaxed, stimulated and focused on the task at hand. This is because Mind Maps contain all the elements of a problem in a single visual 'take', they show you where the real emphasis should lie and are the perfect stress-reducing tool. Add to this the fact that the colour and images stimulate and bring in more of your mental warriors to deal with any given problem and you have a tool that is going both to solve your problem and improve your physical and mental health.

In a situation demanding careful negotiation, the use of Mind Maps encourages radiant thinking and provides endless options, instead of closed confrontational diatribe. Used in conjunction with Mastermind Groups, Mind Maps become even more powerful, helping you to tap into the thinking in some of the world's most brilliant minds.

While there will always be problems cropping up at work, Mind Maps enable you to rise to challenges and display your solution-finding abilities. What may have been seen as simply an obstacle becomes an opportunity to display your creativity. In addition, by using Mind Maps to plan ahead, it is possible to avoid potential difficulties in the first place. This is what we look at in the following chapter.

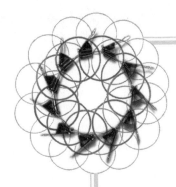

3

Perfect
Planning
for Unlimited
Progress

Planning doesn't have to mean tedious hours with endless notes and documents. With Mind Maps, planning can be fun, easy-to-manage, creative and productive.

When you plan for progress using Mind Maps, you will find it easier and more enjoyable to manage those tasks that you have tended to put off until another day. Not only will Mind Mapping demystify time management and business decisions, you will also find yourself with more time to do the things you *like* doing.

Mind Maps for high-risk investing

Linda Sontag, an investor at Axiom Venture Partners, based in San Francisco, says:

> '*I am a venture capitalist, so my job is high-risk investing. Every week, I see about ten new business plans and visit two or three companies. I use Mind Maps to keep track of whatever it is I'm learning about the individual companies. Mind Maps are the fundamental process by which I make my assessments as to whether or not these*

---

companies are worth investing in or not. I keep very few notes, far fewer now than I've ever kept before, because I'm so used to Mind Maps. The Mind Maps just flow; they've become a part of the way I do business and the way I keep track of the complex companies and industries that I follow.'

As Linda demonstrates, planning is a business tool which can give you a competitive edge and Mind Maps are the clearest manifestation of the process of planning. You can Map anything from your CV to a business plan by using a Mind Map. And, importantly, Mind Maps will help you constantly to re-acquaint yourself with your goals.

BUSINESS PLANNING

Those businesses that plan well are the ones that continue to score highly in consumers' estimations—it is no coincidence that these are the same companies that continue to deliver at the bottom line, year after year.

Gain influence and reduce your workload

Dwain Dunnell, the brains behind the weight-loss system Slimtone, says:

'All my business plans in the past were lists. It's very difficult because the brain doesn't work like a list. If you make a Mind Map for the week or a Mind Map for the day,

> *you can see the route that you need to take to achieve your objective. Using Mind Maps, I did my entire business plan all the way up to £20 million in a year's time, in half an hour. Mind Maps are powerful because they enable us to influence. Influence gives us power and power allows us to achieve our goals. If you can learn how a Mind Map works then you'll learn how your own brain works.'*

Starting a business

Starting up your own business is a daunting prospect. Yet if you are prepared to take the gamble, there are many advantages to going it alone. Although the responsibility is enormous—the buck really does stop with you—it enables you to:

- Control the company's destiny;
- Direct how the company operates;
- Hire your dream team;
- Have the luxury of being able to work where and when you want.

The first step on the road to creating your own enterprise is to Mind Map your business plan. If you want to attract financial backing from a third party, your business plan is a vital tool for wooing potential investors.

MIND MAPPING YOUR BUSINESS PLAN

If you imagine your business is already up and running, this will help you to visualize the business plan much more easily and will assist you in drawing your Mind Map:

1. Put an image representing your business at the centre of your Mind Map. This could be in the form of a company, a picture of the product, or even a brief mission statement.

2. Draw a main branch from your central image and label it 'unique'. Use sub-branches to explore what makes your product or service unique and why you think it would be chosen over the competition.

3. Draw another main branch from your central image and label it 'customers'. Use sub-branches to establish exactly who your customers are, what they want and why your business is what they are looking for. Include here the spread of revenues you expect to receive from different customers. If you can access them, use current financial data from an existing business in a similar line of work to compare and make realistic judgements.

4. Draw a third main branch from your central image and label it 'offices'. Here you can look at the premises you intend to use, as well as the administration, financing and marketing of the company, including details of the costs you calculate will be incurred.

5. Draw a branch from your central image labelled 'structure' to deal with the workforce, including any partners you might have. (If your business plan will be used as a tool to secure venture capital, include the names of your partners and any relevant past experience that they have. It could make all the difference to a venture capitalist wanting to make a sound investment decision.) Using sub-branches, you can investigate recruitment and marketing strategies, along with the sort of team structure you intend to build. This may include different levels of skill and qualification, as well as full-time, part-time, freelance and contract employment.

DEVISING BUSINESS-PLAN HEADINGS

When you come to write your actual business plan, ensure you take the time to Mind Map your thoughts under specific business-plan headings. On a formal business plan—something which you would actually take to your bank manager or a potential investor—your headings should always include the following:

* **Executive summary**—This is a précis of what follows and is normally the last thing to be written in any business plan.

* **Company**—What exactly is your company and what does it offer?

The LadySkillers

Fiona, Susan and Caroline met at a party. Susan had just finished renovating her house and in the process had learnt the basics of building. Caroline, meanwhile, was working as a fully qualified plumber and Fiona was an interior designer. After a few glasses of wine, they had the idea to launch The LadySkillers, a collective of women labourers. The Lady-Skillers would specifically target high-flying and high-powered career women living alone in London who urgently needed jobs doing around the house but who did not want to risk being let down by unreliable workmen. When they discussed their idea again the next day, they realised just how much mileage it had. Their next step was to Mind Map a business plan of the business as if it existed to see if it could work (*see* colour Mind Map of The LadySkillers' business plan).

---

* **Market**—Who is your target market? Are there any other companies out there which you see as competitors? If so, you must face up to this and mention it in the plan. Identify what you would do differently in your company and why this is a unique selling point.

* **Product or service**—What is your product or service and how and when will it be used?

* **Management team**—Do you have partners and if so who are they? What experience do they bring to the equation? If you are aiming to secure venture capital, your people and their business track-record will be the most vital section of your business plan.

* **Strategy and implementation**—What is your long-term plan for the business? Most businesses operate to a five-year plan, although it is not unheard of for this to be reduced to two or three years in the case of start-ups. Be specific about what the company intends to achieve.

* **Financial analysis**—You have to include a financial analysis, particularly if you are presenting the business plan to your bank manager. Make predictions about the financial performance of your company based on solid research and market knowledge. At the very least, this should include 'Profit and Loss' and 'Cash Flow' tables.

Mind Mapping your business plan as if it is an operating business will make the prospect of writing your formal business plan a lot less intimidating. You will have already covered the vital points and feel on familiar ground when the time comes to finalize your plan.

TEFCAS: THE TOOL TO HELP
YOUR PLANS SUCCEED

The TEFCAS success mechanism is a revolutionary business tool because it builds in failure and feedback as two vital ingredients for success. It works brilliantly in combination with Mind Maps: Mind Maps help you plan effectively and the TEFCAS success mechanism helps you monitor and react to the outcome of what you have planned. Both tools help keep you focused on your goals. TEFCAS stands for:

- **T**rial
- **E**vent
- **F**eedback
- **C**heck
- **A**djust
- **S**uccess

Trial

To be a success, in the first place you need to have tried at something. It might be something completely new, or perhaps a different system or procedure.

Whatever it is, if you don't open yourself up to trying in the first place, you will never know.

Imagine you wanted to open up a boutique clothes shop. The trial element would be your research, writing a business plan, going to the bank to apply for a loan to launch your business. It would also be choosing the right clothes, sounding out potential customers and the competition in the area and marketing the imminent launch to the correct target audience. All these are elements that should be included on your Mind Map business plan.

Also to be included here is research into comparable enterprises and the lessons you take from them. It is very useful to speak to people who have set up similar businesses to you. If the enterprise has been a success, they may be more than happy to share their experience with you. Ask them to take you step-by-step through their experience while you draw up a Mind Map with their shop as a central image. This way, you will end up with a true representation of their experience.

Event

An inevitable consequence of your careful planning and subsequent action will be an event. In the case of the boutique, the event is the launch and the first few weeks or months of trading. You could throw a launch party at the shop, inviting people to view the clothes in your shop. You may even make your first sale that night.

The event can be the most intimidating part of the TEFCAS success mechanism. When you get to this stage, there is no turning back. Here is where the confidence and conviction that your venture is a good idea will stand you in good stead.

It will help to keep you focused and boost your confidence to refer back to your business plan Mind Maps now and again to remind yourself of why you decided this venture was a good idea, and the unique aspects that you are bringing to your business. Making yourself familiar with the Mind Maps at the heart of your business strategy will also give you an opportunity to re-acquaint yourself with your short- and long-term goals.

Feedback

Feedback is a vital element in the business world, but it often gets overlooked. It is essential at any stage of an enterprise to know how you are doing if you are going to be able to improve. If your boutique has been going for a month, while in the strictest business sense your takings in the till for that month are the first indication of your success, in fact your primary source of feedback is your customers, so ask them what they like about the store and what they think should be changed.

With this in mind, draw a Mind Map with the customer as your central image and include any of their comments along the main branches. This will be your blueprint for taking your business forward.

The feedback stage would also be a good time to invite contacts you made from other boutiques at the Trial stage to come and visit. Since they know and understand the business, they can offer sound advice.

This is also a timely moment to ask those contacts about any other niggling worries you have. They will feel flattered if you have acted on the advice that they gave you at the Trial stage, so make a point of telling them about any of their tips that you felt were invaluable. Everyone, regardless of wherever they are in their career, is boosted by positive feedback.

Check

As a realist, you completely understand that there is always a process of fine-tuning, if not major change, to undergo. The Check element in the success mechanism is where you make sure you are on track with your original goals, and that the small details of the theoretical model of your business actually work out in practice.

This will be an ongoing process as you continue to develop your project. For instance, in the case of the boutique: is the lighting in the fitting rooms bright enough? Do customers want to pay with a credit card, but you are not equipped to handle it? Do you need to re-stock any items?

All businesses involve checking on a daily basis whether your customers are satisfied or if they are receiving better service elsewhere.

Try to avoid falling into the trap of presuming to know your customers inside-out. If you are in any doubt about what shops they might prefer to yours, then ask them. They will feel flattered, personally involved in your business and, most importantly, they will be much more inclined to return to your shop for that 'personal touch'.

Compare your performance so far with your business goals by Mind Mapping where the business is. You can use the Mind Map instructions for creating a business plan as a guide to help you draw your Mind Map to assess your performance so far. Going through each branch step-by-step will give you a clear idea of where you are meeting your original goals and where you are falling short.

Adjust

In the case of the clothes shop, the Adjust stage is where you can incorporate the feedback from your customers and business acquaintances, as well as put your business back on track with regard to where it is failing to meet some of your original Mind Mapped aims.

For instance, there might be a consensus that the classically tailored clothes you are stocking are not sufficiently exciting or enticing for the catwalk-conscious, cash-rich fashion victims in the neighbourhood. Or it could be that the shop's location is not very convenient for a few of your best customers. To cover this, perhaps you might consider an online shop or a mail-order catalogue. As you understand that any business needs to go through a constant stage of adjustment, then you are already in the correct mind-set. As you make your adjustments, do keep your Mind Maps up-to-date to reflect the current evolutionary stage of your business.

Many businesses have spiralled into demise because their customers' views have not been taken into account. Many of the casualties of the dotcom era were classic examples of companies attracting venture capital and thinking they could change the world. But they neither attracted a loyal customer base, nor listened to their customers and incorporated the feedback into their business.

Success

Your brain wants to succeed and success is the light at the end of the tunnel. The thought of it motivates and inspires you and your determination means that you are destined to get there.

Now you are successful, you may think it is time for a break, time to sit back on your laurels, but you would be wrong. The best businesses in the world are those that enjoy success after success after success. . . . Once they have mastered a core element of their business, they might decide to diversify their offering, using the TEFCAS success mechanism over and over again. In the case of the boutique clothes shop, this could be a second shop, or even a whole chain of shops.

Applying TEFCAS: A different way of thinking

Historically, the businesses which have been the most successful have been those that have offered something new. It might be a radical way of serving customers, such as Amazon.com promising low prices and, crucially, the efficient delivery which seems to elude so many other dotcoms; alternatively, it might be a brand which builds up a market presence and then a culture around that presence. Iconic clothes brands such as Levi's and Diesel are always striving to offer something original and attention-grabbing. Such business successes demonstrate a different way of thinking and you can clearly see how the TEFCAS success mechanism comes into play. When they have reached a successful point, the innovation doesn't stop there.

Whenever you plan anything, be it on a large or small scale, always refer to the TEFCAS mechanism to monitor the outcome of what you have put into practice. This will help you identify any areas of your project that need attention and will give you the greatest chance of long-term success.

PLANNING CVS

As anyone who has ever gone through the process of recruiting a member of staff will tell you, ploughing through endless CVs can be boring. Smart, creative thinkers who take the time and trouble to present their details with imagination and flair stand out from the pile.

Hit the headlines

Tony Dottino of Dottino Consulting in New York used to work for IBM and was responsible for recruiting several team members during his career there. He says:

'In my IBM days, I used to look at CVs coming in and I'd underline key words. I was looking for innovators or energetic, enthusiastic, creative types. And yet, most people are writing CVs that put you to sleep.

'My advice to those people would be to create a Mind Map. I'd want to say to them, "Let's create a picture of what you look like with you as the star of the show! The second step is to branch off five things that you've done that should be on the front page of the Wall Street Journal."

'In my experience, using this process offers a 90% success rate of people getting the jobs they want. Suddenly they have a completely different message!'

Drawing a Mind Map of your CV will certainly help you plan a CV worthy of the *Wall Street Journal*. It will also help you memorize everything on it, making it easier during interview for you to talk about how your experience matches your potential employer's needs.

Depending on the organization you are applying to, you may even want to send in a Mind Map of your CV alongside your conventional CV. A beautifully drawn, colourful Mind Map punches above its weight in terms of presentation. It would be a detailed and well-presented map of who you are and where you want to be, all on one page. Also, it would make you stand out as a creative thinker who is unafraid to do things differently. Every forward-thinking enterprise worth its salt wants to employ staff who fit that description.

MIND MAPPING YOUR CV

1.   Begin with an image of yourself in the centre. This could be a photo, sketch or drawing.

2.   Draw your main branches and label them 'skills', 'experience', 'education' and 'interests'.

3.   Under each heading, go into more depth by using sub-branches. For instance, under 'skills', you could draw branches for 'driving', 'typing', 'shorthand' and 'French'.

4.   Explore each sub-branch by means of a further branch. For instance, from 'typing' write your typing speed and under 'French' write 'conversational' or 'fluent'. Stick to one word per line and don't get bogged down with details. At this stage, your aim is simply to introduce yourself with vibrancy and sparkle.

5.   Draw pictures on your Mind Map. Unless you are particularly artistic, if you want to send your Mind Map to your potential employee, but think it needs to look more professional than a hand drawing, you could use Mind Mapping software such as 'Mind Genius' to re-create your hand-drawn Mind Map.

PLANNING YOUR TIME WITH MIND MAPS

One of the Mind Maps' most important applications in the workplace is in planning your time. Among the most common problems in the tradtional forms of planning are:

- Linear planning that disguises the necessary overall structure of what it is you wish to accomplish;
- Too much emphasis on the short term;
- Failure to recognize true priorities;
- 'Fire-fighting'—dealing with current urgencies rather than the broader themes;
- Uncoordinated approaches, leading to the missing out of vital elements or whole areas that are essential if your plan is to be successful.

Mind Maps can help you avoid these problems, giving you the whole picture, thus allowing you to see both the short and long term.

They also provide an integrated picture that incorporates all the minor and major elements in a coordinated structure. Because of this integrated architecture, Mind Maps also allow you to make more appropriate choices when it comes to prioritization and action planning.

In addition, because of its associated and brain-logical structure, the Mind Map will automatically identify all areas that need to be included in the planning, significantly reducing the likelihood of anything important being left out.

Making proper use of your time enables you to organize your life, giving sufficient space for priority activities and engagements. Efficient time management will result in you having enough time in the day to do your work *and* feel comfortable coping with any last-minute hitches should they occur. This way you will seldom feel stressed out or in a vortex of panic.

SCHEDULING

Everyone appears to have a hectic lifestyle today with ever-increasing demands on their time and this is likely to put you at risk in terms of over-scheduling.

If you were to schedule every hour of every day, you would be short-changing yourself and find yourself with *no time* for outside interests. The brain comes up with its most creative ideas when it is resting and relaxed, but if you have wall-to-wall appointments and meetings, you will be far less likely to come up with original ideas.

Instead of facing a non-stop stream of appointments, engagements and commitments, you can use Mind Maps as your prime time-management tool to help you manage your time on both a macro and a micro level—that is, in the long and short terms.

This will help you focus on your priorities so you do not suffer from a feeling of being squeezed and having no room to breathe.

Planning lessons with Mind Maps

Tom is a secondary-school science teacher in Lancaster. He uses Mind Maps to assess what his pupils know and plan his lessons accordingly:

'As a principle, Mind Maps were introduced to me many years ago. When I started my second teaching job last year, I decided to try using them as a topic starter activity. My experiment was so successful that I have been using them to teach 7–11-year-olds ever since.

'Now, every time I start a new topic I ask my pupils to

---

copy the keyword title of the topic onto the centre of a page and from this draw branches with associated words to detail their current ideas, knowledge and understanding of the topic. Drawing a Mind Map is an accessible but challenging activity, and I find that they really enjoy doing them and are keen to share their ideas in the plenary.

'Moreover, their Mind Maps help me to teach more efficiently and effectively: I can get a good idea of their prior knowledge and understanding of a topic from their Mind Maps and can identify any misconceptions. This means I can plan my lessons according to the individual needs of each class. Mind Maps make my job easier and have helped make me a better, more effective teacher.'

Saving time with Mind Maps: the expert's view

Jeffrey Mayer, the time-management expert and the author of *Time Management for Dummies,* used to be a fastidious note-taker. Now, having realized that Mind Maps can help you make connections between thoughts and ideas, he is a converted Mind Mapper.

He believes that Mind Maps have helped his productivity to soar and uses Mind Maps for everything from note-taking in meetings to organizing material for publication. In his own words:

'Mind Mapping enables me to do in minutes what used to take me hours, sometimes even days.'

He has had his clients taught how to Mind Map too and as a result they have also enjoyed more effective brainstorming sessions, greater ease in meeting deadlines and a fantastic boost to their productivity.

Macro-time management: Mind Mapping your year ahead

You should find the time to review the last 12 months using a Mind Map, including the main events and successes, both personal and professional. This can be an enlightening and intriguing process which gives you wonderful feedback. It is also calming because it enables you to sit back and look reflectively over your memories of that period.

Having completed your review of the year, you can then use it as a springboard for planning your time over the next year.

Mind Map your goals for the coming 12 months—including health and personal development goals, as well as making time for rest and relaxation. Map out an ideal year, incorporating all those elements. By spending some time thinking about exactly what you want from the year, you will be able to set out your agenda—including a little leeway for unforeseen events. In this way you will not be in danger of suffering from burn-out, and will have the satisfaction of achieving your goals.

When you have this broad macro-structure in place, it is easier to go on to prepare Mind Maps for individual weeks and months ahead, along with specific projects which you know are coming up.

Micro-time management: Mind Mapping your week ahead

It is always worth taking time out to Mind Map the week ahead to prevent you panicking at the constant demands on your time.

If you get into the discipline of making a Mind Map for the week ahead, you will also become accustomed to looking beyond each day at a time and what you can achieve in that specific day. The difficulty with many planning tools, particularly electronic ones, is that they remain focused on just the current day. With Mind Maps, you will look at the bigger picture and focus more clearly on your middle-term goals rather than paying attention solely to the next eight hours.

A Mind Map for the week ahead has the added bonus of being able to incorporate priorities from your life outside of work, so that your health and those important events, anniversaries and personal arrangements do not get overlooked as the week rushes by.

In a given week, for instance, you might have several things on your mind. If you were to write a linear list, it might look something like this:

- Girlfriend's birthday, Tuesday
- Dinner party, Thursday evening
- Client presentation, Friday morning
- Interviews for a new member of staff: Tuesday afternoon, Wednesday morning
- Deadline for a preparing presentation: Thursday afternoon
- Pick up cat from vet, Monday morning
- Buy girlfriend's card and present: Monday lunchtime
- Dentist, Wednesday lunchtime
- Team meeting, Monday morning

If you were to draw a Mind Map, however, you would find it easier to juggle your professional life with your personal commitments than if you tried to cope with a linear list. Take a look at the colour Mind Map for ideas of how you can Mind Map your week ahead.

While it may be carved on your memory that it is your girlfriend's birthday on Tuesday, if you have not built time into your schedule to go shopping for a card and a present on Monday, she will justifiably be upset if you are empty-handed on the actual day. But if you use a Mind Map, it will focus your mind on when you can fit everything in. For instance, if you need to book a restaurant table to take your girlfriend out for dinner on her birthday on Tuesday night, your Mind Map will serve as a mental prompt.

Similarly, you have deadlines to meet throughout the week and different work elements clamouring for your attention. Using the Mind Map allows you to plan your workload so that nothing is overlooked. In addition, drawing up your weekly Mind Map will alert you to other Mind Maps that you need to make, such as the one for the questions you want to ask the interviewees you are meeting on Tuesday and Wednesday.

A GOOD MEMORY HELPS YOU PLAN

Remembering what you have planned is just as important as organizing your time or a project. You may not always have your Mind Map to hand, such as in an interview or at an impromptu meeting with your manager by the water cooler, so it is well worth having the information in your head. Knowledge breeds confidence: if you are confident of what you know others will have confidence in you.

The good news is that Mind Maps don't just help you organize yourself and your thoughts but they also make it much easier to remember what you need to know. This is because the act of drawing a Mind Map helps to improve your memory.

For many years, there was a widely held misconception that memory has a finite capacity, much like a computer disk or a hard drive. In fact, it transpires that the more you exercise your memory, the easier you will find it to remember.

The human brain boasts 100 trillion connections joining millions of neurons. Each junction can be part of a memory—physical evidence that the potential memory of your human brain is almost incalculable. The only hurdle you face is storing all this information in the right way. To understand this you have to appreciate that memory is based on two very simple and profound principles:

IMAGINATION AND ASSOCIATION

These are two foundation stones of Mind Mapping, which use a combination of colour, image, individual words and interconnecting branches. Our use of the traditional methods of note-taking has left these two immensely powerful principles by the wayside. But with an increasing understanding that imagination and association are also the driving forces for success in any business, the importance of these skills has become increasingly recognized.

Improving your recall

Read the following statements concerning learning and recall, and see if they apply to you:

'I learn better if I take at least one break every hour.'
'I learn more effectively if something is repeated to me.'
'I learn more about things which are outstanding or unique.'
'I learn less in the middle of a learning period.'
'I learn more at the beginning and end of learning periods.'
'I learn more effectively if things are connected.'

If you reflect on the extent to which you found these statements matched your experience, it may give you some clues as to how you might improve the performance of your memory. It might seem strange, but many people in business possess a very real fear of making their memories work more efficiently for them, preferring to use the traditional methods which they have used ever since their schooldays.

TAKING EXAMS TO PROGRESS AT WORK

Many professions or companies expect you to take exams to advance in your career or become fully qualified. Most organizations expect their employees to revise for these outside of office hours, so it is important that you plan your revision well and give yourself the best chance of success.

One significant problem with revising for exams is that the process can be exceedingly boring, especially when you are tired after a long day's work. Most lecture hand-outs or revision notes consist of black text on a white background. The lack of colour or imagery makes it harder for you to engage your brain, so your memory can became stunted and stuck.

Mind Maps should be your number one revision and exam preparation tool as the way they use colour, image and association tie in closely with the memory principles of imagination and association. They also allow you literally to re-view everything that has been learnt so far—and on one single page rather than hundreds of separate cards or note pages.

In the examination itself, the Mind Map will almost magically appear on your brain's internal screen, allowing you to access the information you have studied almost as if you are back in your study with all the information to hand.

They have been shown again and again to be the most effective way of preparing for exams.

Conjuring up answers with Mind Maps

Dr Reenee Barton, a child psychiatrist in London, has sat exams for over 20 years. Mind Maps have revolutionized her ability to recall facts:

'As a doctor I need to keep passing exams if I want to apply for more senior positions and I have to revise for

---

these in between long working hours. Mind Maps are very useful for consolidating my revision. I have always had a more visual memory, so I found creating Mind Maps a much more stimulating way of studying, especially when I am tired after being on a long shift or on call at night.

'Mind Maps are much easier to reproduce and remember than a list of dry facts. They help me to recall information in a non-linear way, which is essential when I have to write exam essays that require lateral thinking. Rather than having a blind panic trying to retrieve facts from the depths of my memory, I find I can conjure up my related Mind Maps and the information on them. To date I have passed every single postgraduate exam I have taken. Mind Maps have certainly made it easier for me to revise effectively outside of working hours and progress in my career.'

Preventing memory lapses

It is all very well making plans, but sometimes we can suffer from memory lapses at the most inopportune moments. If you have been overworking, your brain can forget the simplest of things.

The suggestions below can all be incorporated into your Mind Maps, making it easier to recall essential pieces of information.

THE VON RESTORFF EFFECT

In 1933, the psychologist Hewig von Restorff published a paper which revealed that we are much more likely to remember an item on a list if it stands out. For instance, if you have a list of numbers with a letter in the middle, you are more likely to remember that letter—simply because it is different from everything else on the list. This is known as the von Restorff effect.

In this manner, you can help yourself remember something by making it bizarre or ridiculous. This way it stands out and is likely to remain prominent in your memory. If you are playful and have fun by using your memory in this way, you will be amazed at what you can remember.

PICTURE THIS

One of the easiest ways to remember is through visualization and imagery. This engages the right brain, so helping the whole brain remember. It also makes using your memory fun and stimulating, rather than a boring endurance test.

Colourful pictures are far easier to remember than words, and you can remember anything by associating it with a vivid image. If your brain makes its own associations, it is more likely to remember things because it has gone through the creative process of linking one thing to another. If you use your creative brain to make the association ridiculous, humorous, outrageous or shocking, then your brain is even more likely to remember it.

MNEMONICS AND MUSIC

Another tried and tested memory technique is mnemonics. If you create a poem, saying or song about the information you want to remember, it is much more likely to be retained in your memory, and more easily retrieved when you need it. Just think about all the hundreds and thousands of songs that are entrenched in your memory. A few bars of the music and suddenly you know the rest of the tune and the lyrics seem to be forming themselves on your lips without any trouble at all.

It is likely that you learned the alphabet, the colours of the rainbow and the number of days in the month by repeating certain songs or sayings. If you apply the same process to remembering more complex data, you will see what a smart shortcut music and sayings can be to aid your memory recall.

A life tool

Approaching memory creatively will pay you dividends in the workplace. You will have information at your fingertips and be the first port of call for clients and colleagues alike. This is because Mind Maps use a powerful synthesis of imagination and association as a tool for:

- Planning;
- Creative thinking;
- Problem solving;
- Project management;
- Self-management;
- Memory.

Mind Maps are the ideal memory tool for both your life and your work. And once you have come up with a brilliant idea, solution or plan, they help embed it in your brain. In business terms, Mind Maps have many Unique Selling Points (USPs).

PLANNING FOR PROGRESS

Mind Maps and the TEFCAS success mechanism can be vital to all aspects of planning your business life. They enable you to:

- Organize your business plan;
- Assess the progress of your plans and identify areas for improvement;
- Create and update your CV in a colourful and visually arresting way;
- Help you plan your time on a micro and a macro level so you don't feel under pressure, enabling you to stay on top of your professional and personal commitments;
- Enhance your memory and stay ahead of the game.

Efficient planning ahead in the short, medium and long term is crucial to any business. When you do this, you will use all the best and most accurate information you have to hand at that time. However, businesses, like all other areas of life, are in a continual state of flux and flow, and what may be a certainty one day, may only be a distant possibility the next. Successful teams and organizations recognize this constant evolution as an opportunity for positive and productive change, and it is to this that we turn in Chapter 4.

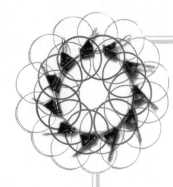

4

Riding the
Powers of
Evolution

As market conditions continuously evolve, a business and the people in that business must also evolve to survive. Mind Maps will give you an up-to-date representation of where you are in respect of your desired career pathway and where your company stands in relation to recent market developments and customer expectation. This will enable both you and your company to determine exactly where you are and what you need to do next. In addition, Mind Maps are the prime tool for enabling fast and efficient reaction to change, enabling you to stay ahead of the game.

Banking on success

Liechtenstein Global Trust, a large banking concern, had the enlightened idea to form an academy to teach all its staff mental, spiritual and physical literacy. As a part of their education, they were taught about Mind Maps. Consequently, these are used at all levels, from manager to cashier, in multiple ways, including:

- **As customer records**—a Mind Map is kept of all prime customers, containing business, professional, career and

---

personal details (such as family and hobbies). This allows them to understand the changing needs of the customer.

- **For making presentations**—both within the company, and at international meetings. Because everyone within the company is Mind Map literate, this doubled the speed of the transfer of information and the acquisition of knowledge.

- **Problem solving**—using their extensive knowledge base, when there is a problem to be solved, each member of the team Mind Maps their ideas, generating between two and ten times as many as they would otherwise. When these are combined in a meeting, new ideas are sparked off, and the best of these are investigated further, allowing the company to adjust to the dynamic business climate.

- **Planning**—each year a Mind Map is made of the company vision for that year. This means that all the team share the same vision and are on task in relation to the next evolutionary phase of the company.

- **Meetings**—Mind Maps are used as the agenda for meetings, the main branches of the Mind Maps representing the main themes. Not only does this help follow the sequential order of points, ensuring that nothing is overlooked, but it also provides an order of significance of the agenda. This is extremely empowering and democratic, as it means that it is the value of the ideas that is important, not the position of the person who comes up with the idea. This is good for the morale of the team and, at the same time, uses the very best ideas from the combined brains in the company.

For LGT, the introduction of Mind Maps has brought creativity and efficiency to the business within an inclusive and vibrant framework.

MANAGING EVOLUTION IN THE WORKPLACE

When a company is going through a period of evolution, it is necessary to think quickly and maintain a flexible outlook, making significant decisions that will affect both the short- and long-term future of your company at a time when you are under pressure.

To facilitate this, unlike with linear-thinking techniques, Mind Maps give you an immediate grasp of any situation that demands evolution. They present an overview that generates options for decision and action.

EVOLUTION IN ACTION

To help you think about the elements that contribute to success, consider the people and businesses that you most admire and reflect your ideas on a Mind Map.

1.   Use a strong central image such as an award or a celebration at work that denotes the success of these companies.

2.   Write the names of individuals or businesses you admire on the main branches stemming from your central image. The individuals can be people whom you know or work with, or business people in the news. The businesses that you use for your examples can be any shape or size, from two people working from a spare room up to a multinational giant.

3.   On sub-branches write the qualities of these individuals of businesses that appeal to you. Stick to one word per line and use colour.

When you look at your finished Mind Map, you are likely to find the same qualities and themes recurring. These are likely to be qualities that you aspire to yourself, or that you know you lack. You may also notice that these individuals and businesses have one other thing in common—they have evolved organically and apparently effortlessly.

Flexibility

Flexibility is a must in your business armoury, preventing you from becoming stuck in a rut, unable to move on and stuck in an outdated vision. By using Mind Maps, you can see clearly where change is necessary and how to move forward in the most positive and efficient manner. If you are proactive and keep your Mind Maps of your position up-to-date, this will enable you to evolve organically, so that change is gradual and progressive, instead of being in a perpetual state of reactive crisis management.

Fear of failure

Many businesses fear change because they are afraid of trying something new and failing. If this is the case, keep referring to the TEFCAS mechanism for success (*see* pp. 51–55). Lessons learnt from failure can become the foundations of success.

You may encounter a few teething problems when you first start to evolve. While you are evolving to adapt to changed conditions, it is inevitable that your new circumstances may take a little getting used to.

However, the alternative to evolution can be extinction. A preparedness for change always reflects a healthy and vital outlook on life, including business life.

Mind Maps will assist you in seeing the bigger picture and the personal and professional contexts for change. They will keep your brain active and alert, while fear of failure can only restrict and subdue it.

KEEPING UP WITH CUSTOMER CHOICE

Customers are spoilt for choice in every aspect of their purchasing, from what car to buy to which supermarket to shop at and what food to eat.

Many factors can influence how they implement their choices. For instance, these may include strong emotional attachments—'Everyone in my family buys Volkswagen cars'; or an ethically conscious approach—'I always buy organic free-range eggs'. Whereas some patterns in purchasing behaviour stay rigidly fixed throughout the span of a customer's lifetime, others are subject to frequent change. In business, it is essential to keep abreast of variations in customer demand.

UNDERSTANDING YOURSELF AS A CONSUMER

Take time to think about what your own purchasing behaviour says about you and the influences that help determine your choices. Draw a Mind Map of those products and services to which you consider yourself to be loyal.

1.   You are the central image in this Mind Map, so put a sketch or photo of yourself in the middle.

2.   Draw your main branches, keeping to one word per line, using the larger purchases you have made in your life, such as cars, kitchen equipment, electrical goods and furniture. Now think of other things that you spend your money on such as holidays, clothes and food.

3.   Explore each main branch in greater detail using sub-branches, including the brand names of the products you buy.

4.   Next, consider why you have written down those particular products. For instance, with 'cars', if you have drawn a few different sub-branches each bearing a different make of car, then consider why you

bought these models. Perhaps a friend owned a car that you particularly admired, or you had recently test-driven that model.

5. Go through the same process with the other branches. Under 'food', you may have dietary requirements or allergies so you hold dear the brands that you trust. Perhaps you have strong feelings about FairTrade, organic and free-range produce. With clothes, it may be there are certain shops that you like because you trust their sizing or find their tailoring flattering to your shape.

Take time to reflect on the choices that have changed over the years. Why were they replaced and what with? Was it a sudden change or a gradual shifting of your loyalties over the years?

This is a useful exercise in helping you understand the many guises of change from a customer point of view. Evolution can be overt or subtle, influenced by advice from friends or family. It can also be informed by a broader perception of a particular company.

Learning to be ready for change

All the best companies are up-to-date in terms of the knowledge (*see* 'Managing knowledge', pp. 134–7) that applies to their product or service. This includes:

- Product developments;
- Market trends;
- Intimate knowledge of the competition;
- Extensive/expansive customer profile.

The accumulation and management of knowledge is at the base of every successful company. This enables them to react fluently and effectively to competition and change. A current strategic and analytic Mind Map of your target customer is essential (*see* 'Mind mapping your target customers', p. 138–40). As your company or the market changes, it is likely you will be able to identify other potential customers and other likely areas of the marketplace.

CHANGING YOUR OWN SITUATION

If you want to change your own work situation, you first need to take a dispassionate look at yourself and determine what exactly it is that you want to change. If, for instance, you 'can't stand your job', what is it about your job that you don't like? Is it the nature of the work, the company culture or do you want more (or less) responsibility? Or are you looking for a whole new career?

Perhaps you think that you are being passed over continually for promotion. Every day, you think you see other members of your team being primed for promotion and you wonder what they are doing right—and what you are doing wrong. Perhaps you have given up, reconciled to the fact that you are never going to progress any further.

Whatever the problem is, it is time to shed some light on the situation. The first step to diagnosing your predicament is to Mind Map your current job and your feelings towards it.

YOUR PLAN FOR PERSONAL EVOLUTION: PART 1

1. Spend some time deciding your central image. The image should reflect your overriding feeling towards your work.

2. Draw main branches which investigate the job, your workload, the nature of the work, the company and the team that you are in.

3. In the sub-branches, go into more detail: it may be that the location of your workplace is getting you down or it could be that there is a more

serious issue emerging. For instance, you may be in doubt about the career path ahead of you and are questioning your long-term commitment towards it.

4. Keep asking yourself questions about the job and exploring them through further sub-branches. Colour code your thoughts and ideas, and use images. This is your blueprint for a happier future, so it is worth investing the time and energy in getting it right.

If you have Mind Mapped your current situation and have now decided that you need to take action, your next step will be to Mind Map what you would *like* to do and to use this Mind Map to propel yourself into a brighter future.

Mind Mapping what you would *really like* to do will make it seem more achievable. Suddenly your world is again full of possibilities and you do not feel imprisoned by your current situation. And by visualizing yourself in the situation you desire, you have taken the first step to fulfilling this.

YOUR PLAN FOR PERSONAL EVOLUTION: PART 2

1. For this Mind Map, use a central image which stands for what you most want from the future. This may be represented by a particular job, by a change of location, a hobby you want to take further, or perhaps by having a family. In the case on p. 82, the image represents a move to France.

2. Explore how you can go about achieving what you want in your main branches: your labels might include themes such as 'training', 'time', 'future', 'money', 'prospects', 'opportunities' and 'goals'.

3. From these main branches, draw sub-branches dealing with the practicalities of the process of your evolution. (In the example on p. 82,

which also includes a 'present' branch which is a reminder of why a move was needed, there is a 'time' branch which is an abbreviated life plan for the coming 3 years; the 'goals' branch is exactly that—in this case representing buying a farmhouse in southern France with a view to doing B & B and lettings, as well as running wine tours; the 'how' branch suggests some of the means of achieving the goals.)

4. If you cross-reference this Mind Map with others you have made, such as your 'work' and 'skills' Mind Maps, you are likely to come up with many more ideas and solutions.

Now that you have Mind Mapped where you want to be, and the route you need to take, the next stage is making it happen. In many cases, this will involve job hunting.

Job hunting

When embarking on a job hunt, it is essential to decide not only what you really want from a job, but what you are prepared to compromise on as well.

If you go back to your Plans for Personal Evolution (*see* pp. 79–81) you will see that you have already identified what you will no longer entertain in a job, what you most want to achieve and what work conditions are essential.

For instance, if you have school-age children and you want to walk with them to school every morning and pick them up in the afternoon, working part-time—or at least having flexitime—will be an essential requirement for any job you decide to take. If you are going to work from home on a freelance basis, you may need to transform one of your rooms into an office. You will need to consider what impact this will have on the rest of the home. For instance, if it is a spare room, will guests still be able to sleep in there when they come to stay? (*See* p. 208 for more on this.)

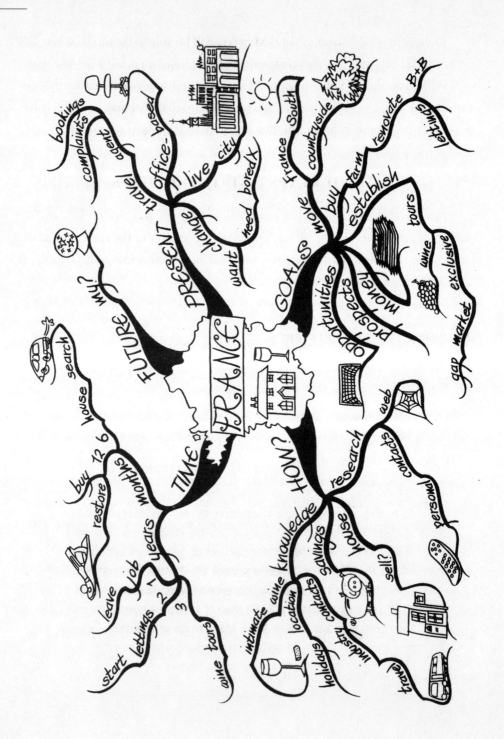

By referring back to your Mind Map you will be able to tackle these kinds of issues at the planning stage so that you can focus more on achieving your goals.

While you should not compromise on your eventual goal, it may be that circumstance and necessities mean that your *route* to that goal may need to evolve. So be flexible where it doesn't matter, but stick to your guns where it does.

MIND MAPS AND INTERVIEWS

Interviews are like a verbal exam where you get the chance to show off your knowledge and shine. If you approach interviews in the same way as exams, using Mind Maps to prepare, you will be overflowing with confidence and enthusiasm (*see* Amir's story).

Planning for an interview

The following story clearly demonstrates how Mind Maps can be the best possible form of preparation for a job interview.

John Mind Maps his way to success

John was applying for a senior position in a large multinational company as vice-president with specific responsibility for personnel and communications—a job he desperately wanted. John was a devoted Mind Mapper and so, when he was preparing for the interview, he drew several Mind Maps. His first was a Mind Map of the company, his second Mind Mapped the job itself and his third was a Mind Map of interview questions. He then prepared two further Mind Maps to do with himself—one revealed what he could do for the company while the other focused on what the company could do for him.

The first question the interview panel asked John was: 'Would you mind telling us about yourself and why you want this job.'

John needed no prompting. He produced his Mind Maps from a folder and showed what he could do for the company. Introducing it, he said: 'I've done a Mind Map to give you a clearer picture of who I am. I've also Mind Mapped the company and the job as I understand it.'

Intrigued, the interview panel looked over John's Mind Maps with interest. As the interview progressed, John referred to his Mind Map when answering each of their subsequent questions. By the time he was showing the interview panel his last Mind Map, the interview had transformed into a conversation about Mind Maps. The interview panel was keen to know more about them and could see the potential for using them within the company. Needless to say, John was employed on the spot.

Researching for an interview

Imagine that you are going for an interview for the job of hotel manager at The Chiltern Hotel. You have already visited the hotel's website, so you know where it is located, how many rooms it has, how many stars it has been awarded and whether it has the facility for additional functions such as conferences and weddings. Look at the hotel's tariffs. How much does a room cost? Make a note of the maximum and minimum costs for a one-night stay. Do these provide value for money when compared with The Chiltern's rival hotels? Incorporate all this information into a Mind Map (*see* colour Mind Map).

Next, you need to flesh out your Mind Map with some additional research before the interview. Try to talk with someone who used to work at the hotel—a present employee might feel compromised and is unlikely to be totally honest with you. It would be ideal if you could find an ex-employee who is aware of how the place is being managed at present. Listen to what is said, paying particular attention to the criticism as well as the praise; this could give you useful material for questions in your interview.

The next step is to go to the hotel. As part of your practical preparation for the interview, time how long the journey takes from your house. Order a pot of coffee in the lobby. Pay attention to what kind of people are coming in and out. Who are the customers? Are they tourists or businessmen?

Study the staff. Are they professional, friendly, helpful? How was your service? How long did you have to wait for your coffee? Did it taste good? Did you have to ask for anything else, such as cream or sugar? Pay attention to such details, always mindful of whether there is room for improvement in any aspect of service, manner and attitude.

When you go home, add the information to your Mind Map. This process will help you to focus completely on the hotel in terms of its strengths and weaknesses, as well as assisting you in understanding where it is in its marketplace and who its competitors are.

Your Mind Map will raise questions that you will want to ask in your interview. It will also highlight how you can furnish some of the answers to the questions that you are likely to be asked. In addition, a Mind Map will help you in terms of practical preparation—such as working out what it will be appropriate to wear on the day.

Preparing for the interview

An interview is a procedure and, just like an exam, once you have done a few, you become accustomed to what is expected of you—and more adept at delivering it. You also become aware that however they are dressed up, there are only a handful of questions in interviews that you are likely to be asked, the five basic ones being:

- 'Why are you in this interview?'
- 'What can you do for the company?'
- 'What kind of person are you?'
- 'What is unique about you which makes you right for this job?'
- 'How much will you cost?'

There are five further questions that may also come into the interview:

- 'Where would you like to be in five years' time?'
- 'What are your strengths and weaknesses?'
- 'How would you describe yourself?'
- 'Why did you leave your last job?'
- 'What do you know about the company?'

The latter question is where your preparation Mind Map really comes into play as it can feed into your knowledge about how you might fit into the wider picture. The information you have gathered can then help to create two further preparation Mind Maps:

MIND MAP 1—WHAT YOU CAN DO FOR THE COMPANY

1. Draw yourself as the central image.

2. Using a single word, label curved branches with the key qualities that you would bring to the job.

3. Explore each of these qualities in depth using sub-branches, saying in what way these qualities would be of practical use to the company.

4. Use images and colour to highlight specific areas.

MIND MAP 2—WHAT THE COMPANY CAN DO FOR YOU

1. Draw an image in the centre to represent the company. Make it relevant to the job you are going for. For instance, if the job is for a teacher in a school, you could draw a blackboard.

2. Draw curved branches off your central image relating to how the job can benefit your life. Focus first on the content of the job and then the workplace environment. Next, think about the big picture, taking into consideration any particular benefits or flexible working conditions that are particularly attractive to you.

3. Using sub-branches, investigate your feelings towards all aspects of the job in question. If you have any doubts or queries about the job, include them.

4. Use images and colour to help you focus in on specific areas.

Revisit both Mind Maps frequently before the interview. You may realize you need to flesh out certain branches of them while you are preparing. With these Mind Maps, you have effectively protected yourself from losing control in the interview. The greatest fear surrounding job interviews is that nerves will get the better of you when you are asked a question which you don't immediately understand. Weighed down by feelings of inadequacy, you feel that you are not capable of giving an appropriate response.

If you have prepared Mind Maps to cover all possible lines of enquiry in the interview, then you have an invaluable tool to assist you in imagining yourself in the interview situation. You will also have the broad picture at your fingertips, as depicted by your research Mind Map. If you do this shortly before your interview, you will be confident that you are prepared for any question. You will be empowered and able to take it all in your stride as you recall your preparation Mind Maps throughout the interview.

Interviewing your interviewer

Remember to interview your interviewer as much as you are interviewed. You need to make sure this job is right for you as much as the company needs to find out if you are the right person for the team. When you are Mind Mapping your questions as part of your preparation, make a point of asking specifics such as about the training you can expect to receive, the promotion prospects there are within the company and the holiday and benefits you would be entitled to. You need to get as much information as possible at your interview so you can decide if this job is right for you.

In the same way that it would be a mistake to make a serious commitment to someone in your personal life who did not feel right for you and whose life visions and priorities differed significantly from yours, apply the same approach to the company where you are going for an interview.

When you arrive for the interview, pick up on any clues as to the company's culture and values. Observe how members of staff interact with each other. Is there an upbeat and cheerful atmosphere or is it more serious and earnest? See what they are wearing and if there is an obvious dress code. Overall, consider from the clues you have managed to pick up whether you can see yourself fitting in.

Presenting yourself

Of course, it will be a waste of all your hard work if you arrive at the interview fully prepared, but then present yourself in an inappropriate manner. Your Mind Maps should give you all the clues you need on the approach to take.

APPEARANCE

How you look in an interview is crucial. You may have spent a week rehearsing your answers for the interview, but if you go in with a suit that is falling apart, the lasting impression your interviewer will have of you is that you do not care enough about the job to make any kind of effort. Remember to include appearance in your preparation Mind Map so that you go in looking your best and wow the interview panel with the effort you have made. This way, in a purely practical sense, your Mind Map will serve as a prompt, reminding you that your shoes need a polish or your hair needs trimming.

BODY LANGUAGE

Your body language also speaks volumes about you. How you walk into a room, how you shake hands, how you cross your legs and what your posture is like. Check everything about your body language before the interview. Make a point of asking friends and family if you have any noticeable habits that you might not be aware of, such as tilting your head or playing with a ring on one of your fingers. If there is anything of this sort that you need to remember, add it to your Mind Map, including an image to reinforce the message.

VERBAL LANGUAGE

Think about how you use language and what it says about you. It does not give a good impression if you always make excuses about yourself ('I couldn't do that because I didn't have time') or be defensive in the language that you use ('It wasn't down to me, it wasn't my responsibility'). It helps to show that you are positive rather than negative, even in the face of adversity.

Employers look for a positive and proactive approach. They want team members who will find solutions for themselves, rather than forever asking others to do it for them. You need to communicate through your choice of language that you are motivated, solution-led and fun to work with. Be definite in the language that you use—and say what you mean.

Employers also look for loyalty. Even though the concept of a job for life is fast becoming archaic, it still pays to demonstrate loyalty. If you left your previous job because you thought your boss was an ogre and you were fed up being ordered about, then avoid focusing on this. If you are quick to be disloyal to your previous boss, your future boss will recognize that there is no guarantee that you will not show the same disloyalty again. Far better to say that you felt you needed new challanges.

At any rate, it pays to let go of negative feelings and show how professional you are in an interview situation.

If you have prepared properly using Mind Maps, you will possess an invaluable tool to help you deal confidently with any interview.

MIND MAPPING FOR A PAY REVIEW

Many employees shy away from asking for a pay rise, even when they really deserve one. Your salary is an integral part of your progress at work, so if you think your performance merits a raise you should be confident about approaching your manager. Mind Maps can help you plan your strategy when you approach your manager:

1. Draw your central image: you can be basic and draw a stack of coins or, more colourfully, a pot of gold at the end of a rainbow. The image should be one that motivates you and makes you more confident when you want to impress your value to the team. It will be this image that is foremost in your mind during your discussion with your team leader.

2. Your main branches should start with 'functions' which will outline your job description, together with any extra responsibilities which you have taken on since starting the job. Explore these responsibilities through sub-branches, making clear how your workload has increased and developed.

3. Another branch will be for the 'accomplishments' or 'success' you have had in the job. Here you can detail instances when you have met particular challenges, completed certain projects or made positive contributions to the company.

4. Next, you should look at how you see your 'future' with the company. Your achievements will clearly demonstrate your strengths and skills, and here you can explore how you would like to develop them further, while indicating how enhancing your role in this way would be of benefit to the company.

5. Finally, it is time to look at your 'value' to the company. This will include not only your past achievements, but also your potential value in the future given your consistent track record, plus your accumulated skills, knowledge and experience. You may actually want to put a figure on what you now consider you are 'worth'; alternatively, you might want to consider who in the company has a comparable role and experience. If you highlight all the reasons why you think you are entitled to a pay rise by means of your Mind Map, at least your manager will have to consider awarding you one.

Resistance is futile

Being rigid and resistant to evolution will mean that your work life will be uneventful, unexciting and, ultimately, unsatisfying.

Conversely, undergoing a process of evolution, however painful or tiring it may be at the time, will make you feel that you have moved on, grown up, acquired more life experience and learnt something about yourself.

Whether it is personal change or fundamental change within a corporate structure, the process of evolution is positive for what it brings out in people. Team members learn a more flexible attitude, companies learn to listen to their customers and atmospheres are renewed and refreshed.

CORPORATE EVOLUTION

Companies change fast. Business decisions are made quickly and staff are expected to keep up.

Mind Maps are the best way for companies to communicate to their staff what changes are taking place along with reasons why those changes need to happen.

Steering through change

1. Firstly, you need to identify exactly how and where the company needs to change. Explore your corporate goals with a Mind Map. This will enable you to see the bigger picture and define exactly where evolution in the company is necessary and what needs to change.

2. Use the Mind Map to communicate the change throughout the company. This will give all team members the ability to understand how the change might affect their individual roles and their relationship with the rest of the team.

3. Use the Mind Map as a focal point for creativity among all staff, encouraging them to come up with suggestions as to how the change might be made easier and more productive and efficient.

Mind Maps for mergers

Recent business history is littered with examples of mergers which were wonderful in theory but catastrophic in practice—usually because although the business reasons looked sound, the fact was overlooked that a company is a community with a distinct culture that is precious to the team that works in it.

A merger is a forging of a new culture from two existing cultures, so it is essential both parties are aware of their own and each other's strengths/weaknesses. Mind Maps are the prime tool for analyzing each other's cultures and defining a new mutual culture. They give an insight into the nuances of the situation, and can root out any potential inconsistencies, contradictions and fault lines. In this way, you can be sure that you share a new mutual vision and there are no undeclared agendas. The essence of successful mergers is integration, not *dis*-integration, which is a symptom of being trapped in a vision past its sell-by date.

1. Mind Map both businesses in separate Mind Maps.

    i) The central image should reflect your perception of the companies. With a strong brand name this might be a logo, or the product it makes. Or it might reflect a positive quality of that company. Write the name of the company alongside the image;

    ii) The main branches will be themes such as staff, location, customers, expertise and profitability (you can follow the template for writing business plans in Chapter 3, *see* pp. 47–8);

    iii) The sub-branches will be the specifics of each area of business.

2. Next, look at the strengths and weaknesses of each business.

3. Create a new Mind Map which draws on the strengths of each business and highlights the potential weaknesses. The use of colours in your Mind Map would be particularly helpful here. (Do not allow forceful personalities or egos to get in the way or dominate this process. This is a sensitive exercise and is not about how one company is bigger or better than the other. Nor is it about who has the most dynamic management team. Learning to co-operate and work harmoniously when working on these Mind Maps will set the tone for the future of the newly merged business.)

When a merger has been completed, Mind Maps, as the embodiment of a shared vision, can then help to embed the new culture and establish beneficial habits of behaviour.

Corporate Social Responsibility

Companies are now under increasing pressure to present a good public face and to be seen to behave responsibly and caringly in the community. This is known as Corporate Social Responsibility (CSR).

Nowadays, consumers want to know that the company with which they spend their money has a caring side and is giving something back to the community and those who need it most—according to one survey, 72% of the public believe that industry and commerce do not give enough attention to the communities in which they have a presence. This is a statistic that could hold the key to the future of your business.

Undoubtedly, being seen to take CSR seriously is good PR, but at a more fundamental level when the company is seen to care about and be closely embedded in the community in which it operates, a more intimate and loyal relationship between company, staff and customer develops. This can only have positive effects on efficiency and profitability.

With this in mind, it would be invaluable to do a self-audit of your company's attitude to CSR, as well as to examine how successfully you communicate this to the wider world. The Mind Map below will help you begin to do this.

BOOSTING YOUR SOCIAL PROFILE

1. Draw a Mind Map with your company as the central image.

2. Draw main branches from your central image which look at ways in which your company demonstrates that it cares about the world in which it operates. The branches could carry words such as 'events', 'recycling', 'sponsorship', 'charity' and 'community'.

3. Spin off themes from the main branches in sub-branches. For instance, from your 'recycling' branch, you could look at recycling paper, cardboard, cans, glass, envelopes and batteries. And growing from your

'events' branch you could explore events such as a tree-planting scheme or visits to the company by local schools.

In 2002–3, the UK's top 100 companies gave 0.8% of their pre-tax profits to good causes. In monetary terms, this came to an estimated £800 million— nearly 2½ times the amount given in 2000–1. The UK government has recognized this and, as a consequence, has launched a CSR academy to promote good business.

Companies which take the trouble to see the bigger picture and actively contribute to the community not only benefit the communities, but also themselves.

A report from The Work Foundation and The Virtuous Circle found organizations that put CSR at the heart of their business strategy could outperform other companies by up to 40%.

Looking at the bigger picture

The short-term view that focuses solely on the next set of financial results is starting to change. Financial scandals at some of America's biggest businesses have led to a call for greater transparency and accountability for both shareholders and customers alike. And it takes more to impress shareholders and potential customers than being photographed giving a cheque to a charity. Significant numbers of investors now pay attention to the ethical track record of companies and time and again a shift in corporate policy has been forced by the weight of public opinion.

MBA courses in the US now include subjects such as sustainability and ecology—and they have come about due to student demand. Younger managers have grown up with significant issues such as global warming and they are eager to embrace these issues in their business lives. The brain-smart companies and leaders are those that embrace CSR and are not afraid to accept the need to evolve the way their company works.

BRANDING

The 'brand' is a term much used in boardrooms, but there is frequently insufficient understanding of what a brand can stand for. Clearly, it amounts to a lot more than a company's logo on a compliment slip or letterhead. The brand creates an emotional association between the consumer and the product or service. This emotional association can form the basis on which the consumer is drawn to buy the product. Beyond this, the brand can signify the relationship between the company, its staff and the community in which it operates. A brand can make a significant impact on a company's share price as well as affecting the bottom line.

If a company is to be successful, it needs a vision, and a brand is a wonderful way of consolidating this vision in the mind's eye. Mind Maps are the ideal tool for focusing on and defining the brand. If each team member Mind Maps what they feel the vision should be, when they combine their ideas on a Mind Map together they will be able to come up with a powerful brand which encapsulates all their aspirations and positive feelings about what they do or provide. In this way, the brand becomes iconic, and what it represents is clearly understood by team members and customers alike.

BRAND AWARENESS

To understand the power branding, think of a brand to which you are loyal and Mind Map it. For instance, if you drink only a certain brand of orange juice, Mind Map that brand:

1.   Draw the product at the centre of your Mind Map

2.   Create main branches from the central image with labels such as 'packaging', 'health', 'convenience', 'freshness' and 'habit'.

3.   Explore each theme in turn using sub-branches. Under 'health', for instance, you may find that you drink a glass of this orange juice every

day because you know it provides you with vitamin C and so helps protect you from colds. Maybe you received that information about vitamin C from the product itself when you were a child. If so, there is a strong chance that this is where you formed an emotional link to it—and it explains the brand loyalty which you feel towards it today.

Apple's new look

Apple is an icon brand which is built around big ideas and which constantly re-invents itself. It knows that Microsoft will always be dominant when it comes to personal computers, so Apple's competitive edge is design. The brand has graced some beautiful-looking equipment which, in terms of aesthetic appeal alone, far outshines Microsoft.

A little-known story about Apple concerns the man given credit with taking the company into the big league. John Scully was the CEO of Pepsi, when he visited the then young and rapidly growing Silicon Valley. When I met him he told me with some enthusiasm how he had toured through the various offices and had been completely stunned by the computer screens. He said that all he saw were lines and lines of rows and rows of screens with lines and lines and rows and rows of words and numbers. He could not comprehend a thing.

This was particularly significant, because John's early training had been in art and design. He knew the importance of image, colour and association. It was this experience—combining the monotony of all the screens with his own background training in art—that convinced him to work with a new company to make screens that were far more brain-friendly. This gave birth to the young giant that Apple became under John's guidance. John's main note-taking technique? He's a Mind Mapper.

PROMOTING CHANGE WITH MIND MAPS: A TALE OF TWO RETAILERSS

Imagine that Dreamworld is a chain of high-street stores offering value for money. It has been going for 30 years, is preoccupied with its historical position in the market and likes to think that it offers something which is tried and tested. Dreamworld is frightened to take risks. It does not believe that it can do anything better or improve on itself in any way, so it sticks its head in the sand and doggedly kids itself that it is fulfilling its potential.

Shopping Paradise is a chain of High Street stores selling similar products at similar prices to the same target market as Dreamworld. It has been around for only 5 years, but is determined to fulfil its potential, capturing as large a share as possible of the potential market. The company uses the collective imagination of the staff to propel them forwards, and the culture encourages an environment in which new ideas are embraced. Shopping Paradise is not afraid to take risks and is in a state of constant development.

The difference between Dreamworld and Shopping Paradise is evolution. While no one would suggest that Dreamworld should undergo drastic or risky change, it should take a look at what it is currently offering its customer—and then try to do it better. Focus groups and consultation with customers could offer insight into where the company is in the here and now, but it will be up to the company to decide how to move forward. (The TEFCAS success mechanism would be of great use here—*see* pp. 51–5.)

Two Mind Maps would help Dreamworld. One Mind Map could mirror where the company is at present. As a team exercise, all of the employees of the company would get together and discuss through the medium of the Mind Map:

- What does Dreamworld do well?
- What is it like as an employer?
- Does it take training seriously enough?
- From a customer point of view, are its promotions getting through to its customers?

Inevitably, taking a thorough look at where a company is will be bound to bring to light areas which need attention, and these need to be noted on the Mind Map.

The second Mind Map will be about Dreamworld in the future:

- What does the company need to do to stay one step ahead of the competition—and, specifically, Shopping Paradise?
- What is the difference for the customer between shopping at the two stores?

Dreamworld has a huge advantage in that it has 30 years of heritage behind it. So it needs to learn from the competition rather than feel threatened by it; in other words, to innovate rather than behave defensively.

Reinventing a Brand

Businesses constantly need to be moving forward, to evolve in response to changing conditions. Attitudes and procedures that were once efficient and innovative can soon become obsolete and old hat. While the central vision behind a brand may remain, the route to achieve that goal may change.

By comparing brands regularly on Mind Maps, it is possible to check up whether your previously perceived strengths are still as strong as they were, or if you are being left behind by events. By constantly checking and adjusting to competition and the marketplace, you will be able to evolve with the times.

However, there may come a time when a more thorough reappraisal is necessary, and you need to reinvent your brand. In order to achieve this, it will be helpful to Mind Map your brand and the brands of the competition (*see* example on p. 101), looking at your relative strengths and weaknesses over a range of issues such as pricing, loyalty schemes, product range, staffing and business location. Next, you will need to reaffirm your goals, in some cases redefining them in the light of changed circumstances. It may be that new products need to be developed, revenue increased or the premises modernized. In the case of Black's Pharmacy shown opposite, these goals are to increase their turnover by 24 per cent, to modernize their shabby premises, to set up an on-site clinic offering complementary treatments and to use this service to go into partnership with a nearby doctor's surgery. Lastly, a plan of action needs to be drawn up outlining how your new goals are to be achieved. Black's Pharmacy intend to action their goals by converting their premises, improving staff training, recruiting practitioners for their clinic and establishing an ongoing programme of research.

A business should always aim to involve all the team in its process of change, as this will maximize the number of creative ideas that goes into it. Also, you will then all share and own your renewed vision for the future.

TECHNOLOGY AND CHANGE

Technology is often cited as the reason for the present fast pace of change in the business world. Yet, in reality, it is people's capacity to embrace change and progress which has been the main catalyst for technological advance. A vivid testament to this was the embracing of steam power, adapting it for every conceivable purpose, during the Industrial Revolution. In a similar way, the development of computer technology has opened up wide avenues of potential innovation. But no sooner than a technological need has been fulfilled, another is identified. This constant cycle of innovation and demand is a case study of evolution in action.

A significant portion of modern business life is spent devising ways in which technology can assist the brain in making everyday business tasks smoother and more economical. This has the effect of freeing up more time and resources to focus on customers.

Successful companies are those which enable their consumers to hold them to account—and feel comfortable in doing so. This is a most satisfactory relationship as consumers dislike being dictated to, preferring to feel empowered;

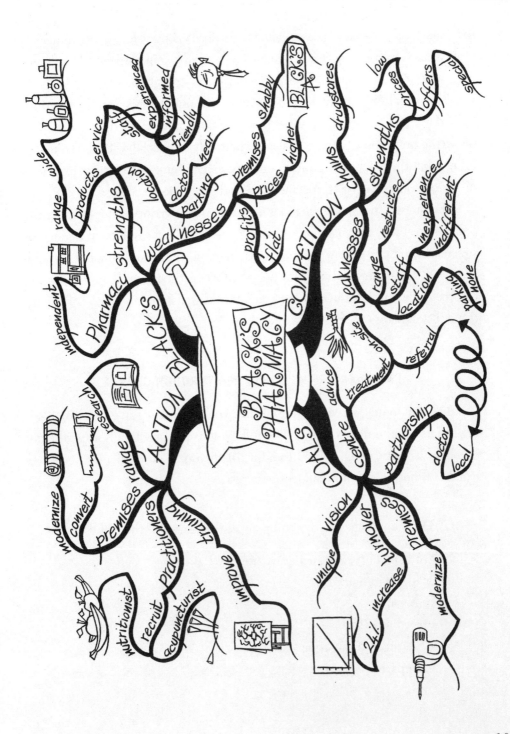

for its part, the company is given valuable feedback about what the customer actually wants. In fulfilling these demands by evolving some aspects of the company strategy, a mutually beneficial relationship is strengthened.

Company loyalty cards have become much more sophisticated since their early days, technological advances now enable highly detailed customer profiles to be developed. Again, this can be mutually beneficial, with the company clear about the customer requirements, as well as being able to target sections of the customer base with special offers and promotions.

The internet has also changed purchasing patterns due to empowering the online consumer. When shopping online, an individual can look at a range of sites and products before making up their mind, just like browsing through several different shops, but from the comfort of their own home. However, the customer still has the option to go out to shop, so the influence of the internet is felt across the whole marketplace.

EMPOWERING THE CONSUMER THROUGH CHANGE

It is vital to make a Mind Map of how your company can create that feeling of customer empowerment. The following is a suggestion how you might go about it, but it is up to you to adjust it to your own particular needs. As usual, it is best if all your team contributes.

1. Draw an image of your company at the centre of the Mind Map.

2. On main curved branches, write:
   a) loyalty schemes,
   b) rewards,
   c) customer service,
   d) shorter waiting time,
   e) impartial advice.

3. Explore the feasibility and possible consequences of offering each 'empowering' service.

4. Use coloured numbers to prioritize those services which you think your customers would respond towards most positively.

As we have seen, evolution at work is a must for company survival and success. And integral to a successful company is a happy workforce. Change is in the natural order of life, but it is our attitude towards it that marks us out. For some, change is something that preferably would be ignored, but which is grudgingly acknowledged and accommodated.

For others, change is at the heart of the vibrancy of life, forever bringing new experiences and opportunities. Mind Maps are the ideal tool for all of us to understand the changing circumstances around us, and then to embrace the new openings that are being offered. As such, Mind Maps are the tool of choice for all successful team leaders, as you will learn in the following chapter.

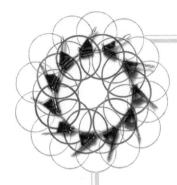

5

Leading
Your Team
to Success

G ood managers can make the difference between a team that succeeds and a team that fails. This is why the best managers need to manage themselves with as much skill as they manage the people under them. Mind Maps and the TEFCAS success mechanism are your key allies in focusing your leadership skills and leading your team to success.

START WITH YOURSELF

Before we take a closer look at the dynamics of good leadership ask yourself the following questions:

- What do you think makes a good leader?
- What kind of manager do you think you are?
- Do you think you set your team a good example?
- Which of your managers, past or present, do you most admire and why?
- How well do you cope in the face of a team crisis?
- Do you encourage transparency and communication?
- Are you quicker to praise or to criticize?

Knowing yourself—your strengths and your weaknesses—is your key to becoming an effective leader.

WHAT MAKES A GOOD MANAGER?

1. Draw a central image that is relevant to the team you manage. You could draw your team logo or sketches of your team members as shown in the example opposite.

2. Next draw your main branches and write on them what you think are the key principles of being a good manager. Who and what do you have to manage? One of these branches should include you. In the Mind Map opposite, the key principles identified are 'self', 'staff', 'product' and 'environment'.

3. Explore your main branches and develop your Mind Map, adding as many sub-branches as you need. For example, what aspects of yourself do you have to manage? Your workload? Your knowledge of your clients, staff or product? Do you have to manage your skills and keep up to date with the latest market developments?

4. Keep this Mind Map with you as you read through this chapter. Develop it further as you gather new ideas of good leadership.

MANAGING YOURSELF

As a team leader your first priority is to be able to manage yourself: you need to set your team a standard. For this, you will need to:

- Organize your own time, schedules and workload;
- Make knowledge your priority, be it of your company, team, client-base, market or product;
- Always seek to build your skills and improve your systems;
- Look after your health and fitness and minimize stress levels.

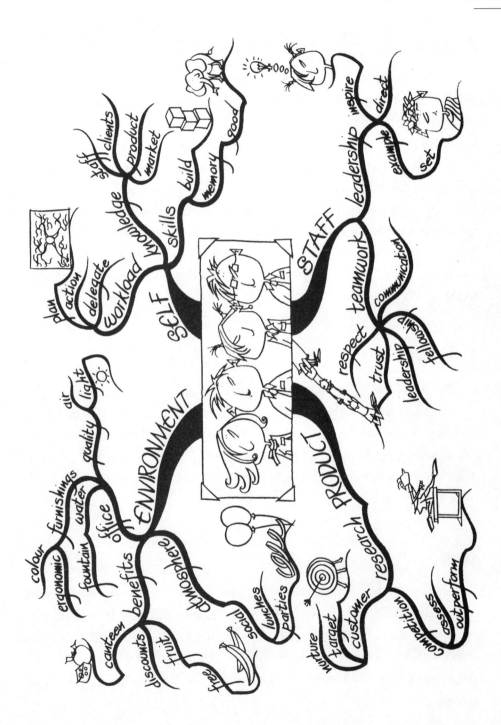

Planning

As we have seen in Chapter 3, 'Perfect Planning for Unlimited Progress', Mind Maps are invaluable both for short- and long-term planning. Whether planning for the coming week, month or year, Mind Maps will allow you to structure your life, so that you can achieve the most without stress or disruption. If you are poorly organized, you can create a permanent atmosphere of crisis which is not only unsettling and stressful, but also unconducive to creative work. If it happens that you do Mind Map your time, but still never seem to be able to fit everything in, the chances are that you have not learned how to delegate, to entrust tasks to others who may be equally, if not more, capable of completing them (*see also* p. 40). This is a valuable lesson to learn.

Knowledge

To be an excellent manager you need to be able to gather and assimilate relevant facts and knowledge with ease. When you are making creative decisions, the more facts and knowledge you have at your fingertips, the more information your brain will have to use when coming up with a solution. Also, mastering detailed knowledge of your customers can pay dividends (*see* p. 137).

Skills

Always seek to improve your skills base as the chances are it will widen your horizons and make you a better leader. Use Mind Maps to regularly review your systems in place at work to see if they can be improved upon. The secret is always to look for opportunities to improve performance, both yours and that of your team. The best leaders will always spot areas for improvement and take action.

Health

A leader needs, as far as possible, to stay fit and healthy. Too often, managers will cut corners with regard to their personal needs. It may be that they stay too long at work, don't bother to take breaks or eat sensibly and, perhaps, smoke and drink too much in a short-term effort to counteract stress caused by their poor organizational skills. In fact, when Mind Mapping your time, you should always make sure that you allot space for looking after your own needs. The importance of maintaining a good work–life balance—and how to go about it—is described in detail in Chapter 8, 'Work–Life Balance Solutions'. Suffice it to say, if you are able to keep your work life in its place and enjoy a relaxed and active time away from work, you are likely to make a much better leader.

LEADING YOUR TEAM

A team is a group of individuals working towards a common goal. This sounds like a simple concept, but it is not always as simple in practice, as the Olympic story below demonstrates. Without good leadership a team will often lose sight of its vision and begin to fail. Much of what comes down to encouraging your team to work well together is similar to good interview technique:

- Listening and speaking an equal amount;
- Showing interest in people and ideas;
- Having a clear idea of where you, the team and the company are all headed.

Mind Maps can help your team to focus on the way ahead and unite you with a shared, creative and imaginative vision.

Mind Maps: The oracles at Oracle

Alan Matcham is a director at the multinational software giant Oracle, EMEA industries. He says:

'Mind Maps have permeated Oracle. They are part of a drive for greater innovation within the company. We characterize ourselves as being efficient, but with a need to be more effective and there are huge differences between the two. Mind Maps, though, have enabled us to improve our effectiveness. As I look around Oracle, there are many individuals who go about their business using Mind Maps. I use them to run my own life within Oracle and I am not alone. There are a lot of people who use them to organize and orchestrate activity. We are a complicated business so Mind Maps help— I could not manage the complexity of my work without Mind Maps. I have often used Mind Maps to deal with the complexities of how we should move forward. Frankly, they are invaluable.'

Opposite is a perfect example of how Mind Maps can help you and your team focus your vision, define the tasks for each individual and drastically improve your performance.

You can use Mind Maps to refocus your team in a number of ways. For example, you could start by getting each team member to Mind Map where they think you as a team, department or company are going and then discuss everybody's opinions on a meta-Mind Map.

Visions of glory

As the Olympic Games in Seoul were drawing near, I was approached to help coach an Olympic rowing squad which was experiencing difficulties so severe it was in danger of being dropped from the team. The members of the squad were all over 6ft tall, had been training for four years, had rowed at international level and were vastly experienced. What could possibly be going wrong? To find out, I asked them the following questions:

- *'What are your personal goals within the team?'*
- *'What do you think other people's goals are?'*
- *'What do you think are the two main strengths of the team?'*
- *'What do you think are the two main weaknesses of the team?'*
- *'Which teams do you think will win the gold, silver and bronze at the Olympics?'*

The answers were fascinating:

- *Each of their individual goals were different;*
- *None identified accurately anyone else's goals;*
- *The number of strengths they identified were many; the number of weaknesses were only two—no commitment and no power;*
- *They all predicted that other teams would win the gold, silver and bronze (with the exception of two wags who said that they would win a medal—but said it only as a joke).*

> The Mind Map of their mental state showed that they were united in their lack of common vision, in their unanimity concerning their weaknesses and in their total agreement that they didn't stand a chance. It was not surprising that they weren't performing well.
>
> We adjusted their thinking so that the Mind Map transformed it into one of common assumptions, shared knowledge, complete commitment and an identical vision.
>
> As a result, in a mere three months the team went from ranking around 50th in the world to an unexpected 4th place finish in the Olympic final.

Alternatively, if you want to implement changes in the department you can call a meeting and use a Mind Map to explain what these changes are, how they will improve your department and how you will go about implanting them. You can then post your Mind Map on the wall so that your new vision remains an ongoing priority in the minds of each team member.

For more advice on using Mind Maps in presentations, see Chapter 7, 'Presentation Power'.

MANAGING CRISES

All managers have to cope with a crisis at some time or another. You may have to manage a power failure or a systems breakdown at a crucial time in your business cycle. You may also find yourself responsible for telling people that they are to be made redundant—possibly the most stressful ordeal that a manager will ever have to go through, especially if those workers have families to support.

But, nevertheless, redundancy is a fact of life. In 2002, 1.3 million employees of Fortune 500 companies lost their jobs, demonstrating that it is not only smaller companies that are at risk from the vagaries of the economy.

The news will not only affect the people being made redundant, but also the rest of the team. Draw a Mind Map of the team and make the key people in that team the main branches. This way you can anticipate their reactions to the redundancies. You will be relying on them to support the team, so it is important to consider their feelings.

Preparing for redundancies

Before you have to break the news, ask around and see if there are any other jobs available either inside or outside the company. If there are, Mind Map them to see which might be suitable for those with particular skills or interests. Make sure that you are ready to maintain an open and honest dialogue with those who are about to lose their positions and they will be more inclined to understand why you are having to take this action. Throughout the entire process, make sure your mutual respect stays intact and that the employee understands that it is a business decision and nothing personal. To this end, Mind Map the situation so you are able to respond calmly and sensitively to whatever arises.

Redundancy

People respond differently to redundancy. If one person might have been thinking about leaving anyway, they might view their redundancy as an opportunity rather than a crisis; for another the news might leave them feeling distraught, depressed and disillusioned about their own ability.

Keeping control in a crisis

If you are using the TEFCAS success mechanism (*see* Chapter 3, pp. 51–5), then you will not be defeated when something doesn't work perfectly first time round. Instead, you will know that you have to analyze the situation and make some adjustments before it works out.

It is the same during a crisis, only you need to think and act quickly, creatively and flexibly. A sure-fire way to help you act with precision, focus and energy is to keep Mind Mapping. This way you are in control of the situation rather than it controlling you.

CONFERENCE CRISIS

Imagine you are the manager at an events company. It is the day before your most important conference of the year and you have just heard that two of your star speakers have gone down with the flu. They are the biggest names on your programme and you marketed the event around them. How are you going to break the news that they are not appearing?

1. KEEP CALM

Panic instantly blinds you to the bigger picture and leads to your brain seizing up. If you feel yourself becoming gripped by panic, walk away from the situation for 10 minutes. Creating distance between yourself and the immediate challenge confronting you can only be beneficial. If you are too emotionally tied up with the situation, you are more likely to make a hasty knee-jerk decision, rather than a responsible course of action. Consequently, your reputation as an excellent events manager will not be enhanced. If you take the attitude that this is not a problem but an opportunity to display your solution-finding skills, you are far more likely to come up with creative answers.

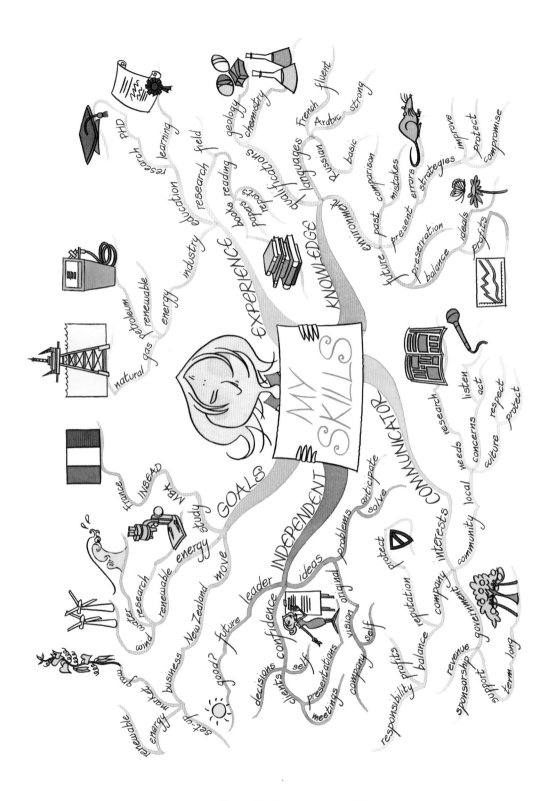

Your Key Skills (see p. 11)

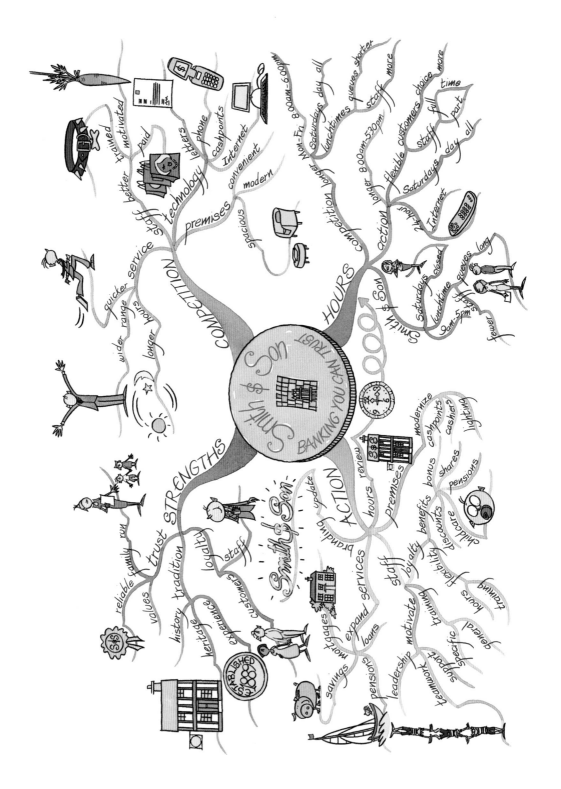

Solving Long-term Problems—Smith & Sons (see p. 32)

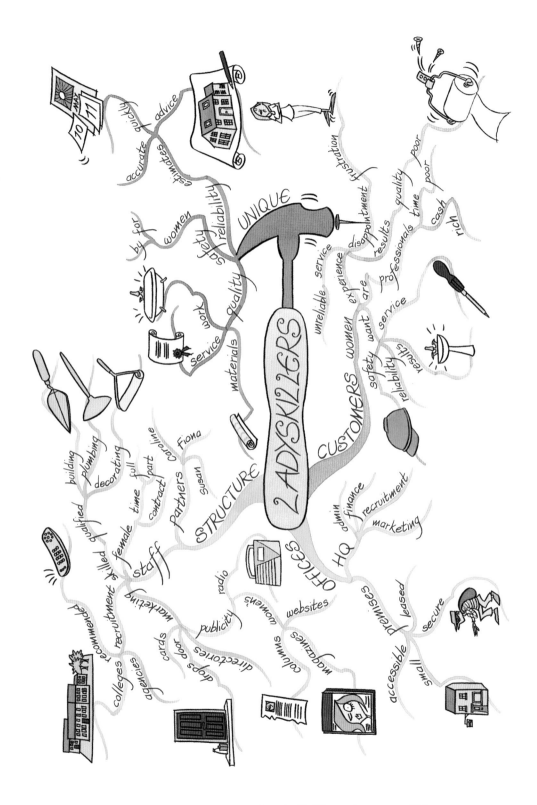

Planning a Business—LadySkillers (see p. 49)

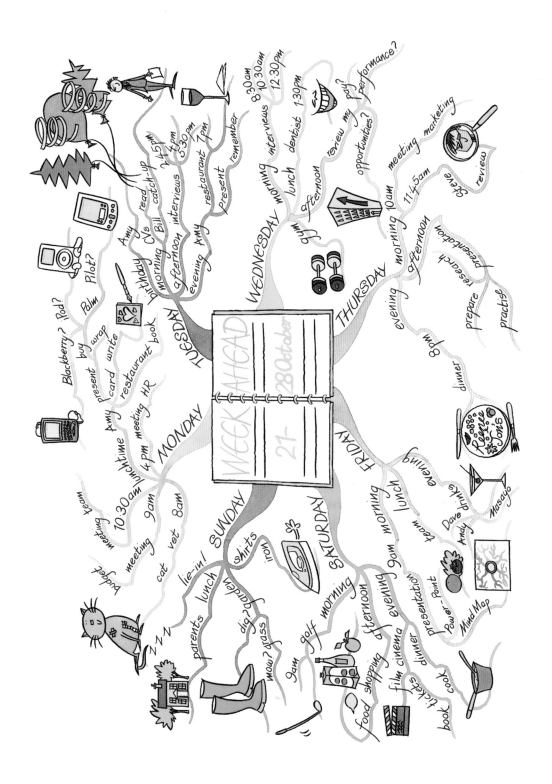

Planning Your Week Ahead (see p. 61)

Researching for an Interview (see p. 84)

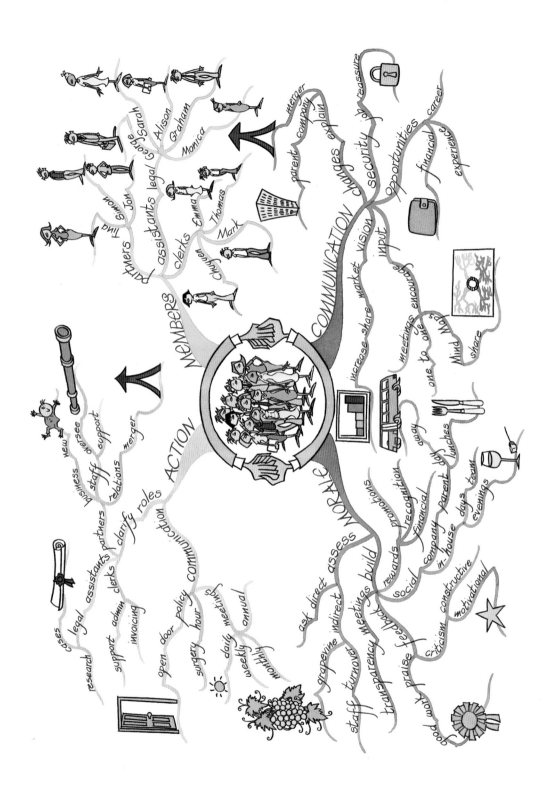

Building a Future Together (see p.125)

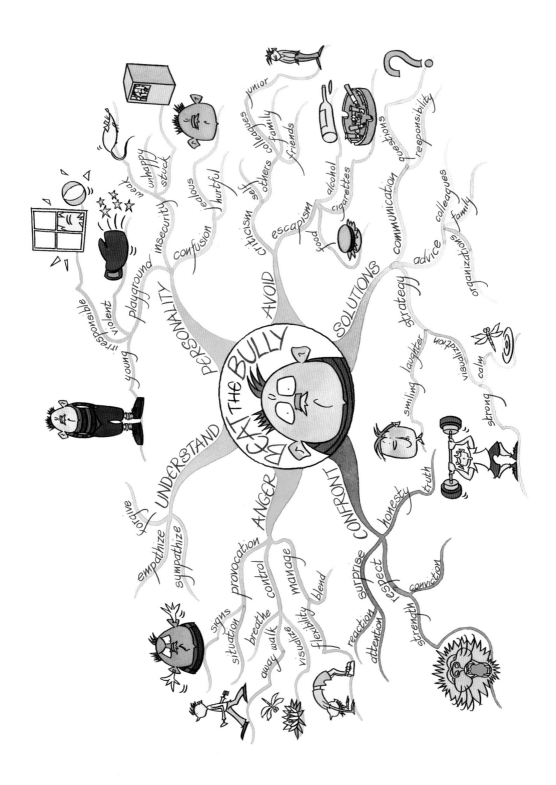

Beat the Bully (see p.161)

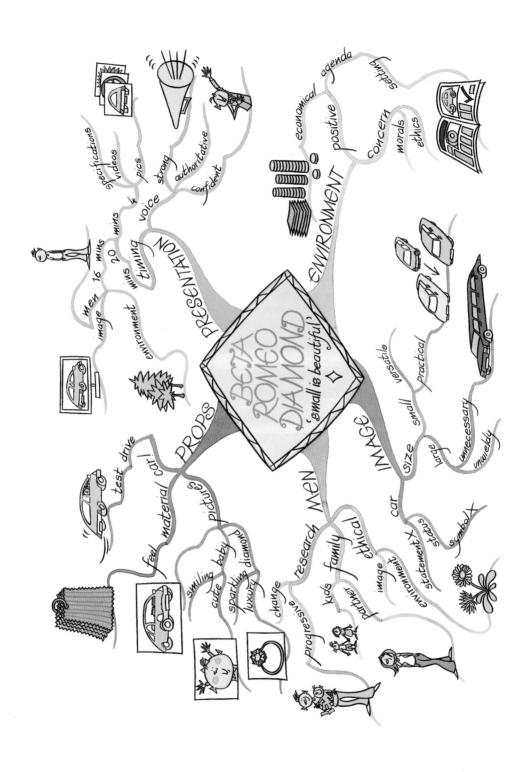

Presentation Power—Beta Romeo Diamond (see p.181)

2. REVISIT YOUR MIND MAPS

When the conference was at the planning stage, you held Mind Map brainstorming sessions to work out the content and the speakers. Refer back to those Mind Maps to see if there are any other names that you could fill in. Perhaps there is someone you might be able to call on at short notice.

3. MAKE YOUR DECISION

Mind Map all your options and order them in terms of preference using coloured pens. Phone around and see who might be available, making notes on your Mind Map as you go. Appointments are cancelled, rescheduled and re-arranged, business trips get postponed or scrapped and deadlines are lengthened. You may be surprised at the top names you are able to net with just 24 hours' notice. Apply yourself and motivate your team to go for the big names, the expert speakers in the field. If expectations have to be lowered, then they can be lowered in the positive knowledge that you have explored every avenue.

Mind Maps help you to apply a creative methodology to the situation in hand. The team knows what it is doing and you are calmly steering the ship through the storm. A good case in point concerns my own learning and thinking courses for Management Centre Europe (MCE).

Smart-brain move

On the first evening of a two-day seminar, I had booked an international chess Master to play 20 simultaneous games of chess against the delegates, in order to demonstrate to them the power and potential of the human brain, with particular reference to the powers of concentration, work ethic, memory and creative thinking.

Five days before the event, the international Master came down with flu and was told by his doctor that there was no way he would be able to make the event. The organizer telephoned me in a panic because there was 'no time' to find a replacement. Of course, there was time—there were five days.

I told her to pursue every avenue—and in the end the solution came from a most surprising source. Over afternoon tea with some friends, at which her seven-year-old son was present, she explained, almost tearfully, her dilemma. Suddenly her son piped up, 'Mummy, why don't you try Raymond Keene?'

Not having the faintest idea who Raymond Keene was, and egged on by her son who had become enamoured of chess at his school chess club, she contacted Raymond Keene and asked him if he could possibly fill in for the missing international Master. Mr Keene said that he could.

She then nervously telephoned me and asked if I would be willing to accept this unknown chap called Keene as a substitute. I nearly fell off my chair. I told her that it was as if she were asking me whether I would mind, instead of having the amateur lightweight boxing champion from Scunthorpe, having Mohammed Ali as his substitute.

Raymond Keene is one of the greatest chess Grandmasters to have lived. He has written more books on chess and thinking than anyone in history (over 110—and still counting), is the Chess and Mind Sports writer for *The Times* and the *International Herald Tribune,* and is arguably the greatest simultaneous chess player in the history of the game.

The lessons to be learnt from this story are:

- There is always a solution to a problem;
- Crises need to be looked at as opportunities;
- Crises should galvanize you to action and stimulate your creative thinking;
- The solution to a problem is often an improvement on the situation that existed before the problem arose;
- Crises help you break unthinking habits of behaviour;
- Giving up is the only guaranteed method of losing;
- Solutions to problems will often come from the most unexpected sources;
- In problem situations, keep your eyes and mind wide open and expand the membership of your team;
- 'It's not over until it's over'—and even then it's not over.

To emphasize the point further, the following story dramatically demonstrates how Mind Maps can help in even the most extreme crisis.

A phoenix from the ashes

Sami Khan, vice-president of Veritas DCG in Singapore, recounts:

'About eight years ago I was travelling to Singapore after a business meeting. During the journey, I received a voicemail saying the office had burnt down. Immediately, I went to the office and, although one part of the building was still intact, the entire computer centre was burnt to the ground. Luckily, it had happened on a

---

Friday night/early Saturday morning so no one was in the building.

'Our regional manager, myself and all the senior managers were there. We had to inform our headquarters and our chairman in the US and our emergency-response plan swung into action. We salvaged whatever we could in terms of the data because a lot of that data belonged to the customers—major oil companies. We went into areas ankle-deep in water and soot and tried to salvage the tapes, which we did all Saturday and Sunday. By Monday morning, our chairman arrived in Singapore and we had a meeting about what we were to do and how we were going to plan to rebuild the operation.

'On Monday we decided that all the employees should go home except for the key people we needed to build the place together. We convened that same evening, Monday evening, at one of the local hotels and asked the employees to come to a Question and Answer session. The chairman's opening remark was that we were going to build a bigger and better operation. Some people felt that the company might just take the insurance money and close the operation down completely which was not the case.

The key employees were told who was needed to come to the office to work over the coming weeks. On Tuesday morning, the chairman, who was driving the whole process, started to get hold of flip-charts and markers to work out a plan and Mind Map who was going to do what. And there was a place for reporting at the end of the day where we were in relation to where we think we should have been.

> '*My job was to take care of all the public-relation issues and to contact each of our customers on the telephone and advise them of what had happened and how we were going to fix it. The chairman took on an organizing role. There was a task force to work out what we could salvage. Then there was an engineering group which laid out how they would rebuild the computer centre. Basically, we Mapped this out every day right down to the cleaning of the office, re-carpeting the entire office, fumigating the building, so that when people came in two weeks' time, business as usual.*
>
> '*This went on every day, and it was incredible how in a crisis people came together—the organization was like our own family and we had to work to try and get over this no matter what.*
>
> '*So we Mind Mapped every process and, would you believe it, in a matter of 10 days we brought the entire computer centre up and into full production. Mind Maps saved them an estimated US$3–4m. If you look at our operation today, it has grown over the last eight years and has made us from being number three or four in this region to number one in this region today.*'

COMMUNICATION

The best leaders are those who have the big, visionary ideas and know how to communicate them well. The more you can encourage good communication on every level—within your team, throughout your company and with your customers and outside agencies—the more effective a leader you will be.

Mind Maps can be key in communicating clearly, avoiding misunderstandings and settling disputes. The following story is a dramatic example of this.

Communication, not conflict

In November 2003, Mexico was hosting the World Trade Organization (WTO) annual conference in Cancun. The previous WTO meetings, and in particular the one in Seattle, had attracted anti-globalization protests which had made headline news in 2001. In Mexico, anti-globalization protestors had promised disruption on a grander scale than Seattle.

The Mexican government and military, in conjunction with the Mexican security company Vitalis, decided to Mind Map all possible tasks that could take place during the week of the conference. Some 8,829 tasks were identified and Mind Mapped in a meta-Mind Map. They then Mind Mapped all possible areas of conflict and the ways in which they could be contained peacefully.

Next, they Mind Mapped the plans and intentions of all the anti-globalization protestors, and contacted those organizations and showed them the Mind Maps with the aim of breaking down the 'them and us' barrier. Rather than have the protestors disrupt the livelihood of people in Cancun, the Mexican authorities in charge of the conference promised them accommodation and time with the media to present their case. So what happened next?

- The event went off without a single act of violence of one person against another;
- There was extraordinary co-operation between previously opposing factions;

> - The leaders of the anti-globalization movement expressed their appreciation at what the organizers of the WTO conference did for them;
> - A 200-page document based on how Mind Maps were instrumental in the planning and implementation of the event was prepared. That document is now used as an operations manual and blueprint for how to manage other major international events facing a similar threat of violence.

As well as being a particularly striking example of the use of Mind Maps, this story also demonstrates some other qualities which are essential to good business:

- Listening;
- Planning and adjustment;
- Open-mindedness;
- Persistence.

It is also a perfect example of the TEFCAS success mechanism (*see* pp. 51–5) in action, proving, most crucially, that lessons learnt from failure lead to success. In this case, the failure of the conference organizers in Seattle to contain the violence in that city had led to a renewed and ultimately successful approach in Mexico.

Communicating difficult news

Whether you have good or bad news, your staff will want to be kept informed. If it is bad news, then it is probable that the rumour mill will already be going into overdrive which can be even more damaging to staff morale.

If tough business decisions have to be made, you will find it easier to talk through them with your team by using a Mind Map. Mind Maps help to put any situation into a clearer focus. They help to quash hearsay by presenting the facts clearly, showing how they impact on each member of the company.

For instance, if pay rises have had to be frozen for the second consecutive year, sharing the reasons behind financial data through the medium of a Mind Map enables team members to put the situation into context and often will inspire them to bond together and throw more energy into their efforts, as was the case for the restaurant chain Mex.

Mex spices up its act

Mex, a Mexican restaurant chain in the southern US, was in dire straits. In fact, it was within three months of going into bankruptcy. The company director Mr Liuzza brought all the staff together—waiters, cooks, washers, cleaners and managers—from each of the company's 10 restaurants, and put the situation to them bluntly. If matters didn't improve very quickly, the restaurants would close and they would all be out of a job.

Together, they made a giant Mind Map of what the current problems were, and then went on to have a brilliant brainstorming session to find possible solutions. Eventually, they came up with some ideas, like redecorating the premises, wearing uniforms, and even *employing another person*, to stand outside the restaurants, welcoming customers with a big smile, and making them introductory offers such as a free canapé.

During this difficult time, not one single employee left the company, and some even volunteered to take temporary wage cuts. Through sheer hard work and team spirit, founded on superb morale, the fortunes of Mex were turned around within 2 months.

RALLYING YOUR TEAM IN DIFFICULT TIMES

Try to communicate news or changes that are going to affect everybody as soon as possible and call a meeting to replace rumour with facts. Prepare a Mind Map in advance and use it to explain the changes that will take place and how this will affect everybody.

1.   Start by drawing a central image that is meaningful for your situation. The example in the colour Mind Map 'Building a Future Together' is a scenario of a legal firm that has just merged with another larger firm and has the team members as its central image.

2.   Next draw your main branches for the key points of the news that you need to share and how this will affect your staff and/or company. The Mind Map identifies 'members' (the people who will be affected by the changes), 'communication' (what will need to be shared with the staff), 'morale' (the key issue at stake to retain staff) and 'action' (the action that the staff and company need to take).

3.   Develop your branches with as many sub-branches as you need. For example, if people are leaving and morale is very low, how are you going to rebuild it? What sort of incentives can you give your staff to stay? Do you have a culture of negative management, where your managers are quicker to criticize and blame than they are to praise?

When you have explored all the possibilities on your Mind Map, use it to structure your presentation to the team. (For more information about using Mind Maps in presentations see Chapter 7, 'Presentation Power'.) Your staff will value your honesty and the chances are that the reality is far less worrying for them than their speculations.

EFFECTIVE PEOPLE MANAGEMENT

What makes you want to do your job? What keeps you there? The chances are it is for one or more of the following reasons:

- You face fresh challenges daily;
- You feel valued and appreciated;
- You are rewarded financially;
- You get positive feedback from your colleagues;
- You feel you are making a difference;
- You have a good work—life balance.

The key to managing people at work is to work out what motivates them and to use that information to bring out the best in them. For example, some people enjoy the thrill of change and uncertainty whilst others yearn for the security of unchanging routine. This is why different people are suited to different jobs and tasks.

Motivation should always be at the forefront of any manager's thinking. If, as a team leader, you show enthusiasm and passion for your business, this positive energy will permeate the workplace. This is not to say you should expect everyone to revel in the more mundane aspects of a task, but if Mind Maps are available to show how each aspect of a project contributes to a creative outcome, some element of job satisfaction will be attained.

If, however, you can motivate your team to motivate themselves, you are going one step further by empowering them. Put time and energy into building up their confidence so they feel good about what they do. They will then bond together more closely as a team. Encourage your team to feel proud of their accomplishments and creativity and make them appreciate the processes they developed to help achieve them.

It is this confidence-building which will help construct and reveal the next generation of management. It is important for managers to nurture the future leading lights of their companies.

Maintaining your staff motivation

A report by Hewitt Associates, a global consultancy, includes the following tactics for maintaining the loyalty of your staff:

1. Look at your managers—If their attitude is cold and un-caring, then team members will feel unconfident and un-cared for—and may leave. A cold, inflexible attitude is not tolerated in lower-ranking staff members, so neither should it be acceptable among those higher up the corporate ladder. The impact a negative and difficult manager has on the rest of the team should never be underestimated. If this is a prob-lem, then it needs addressing right away.

2. Have a clear-cut mission—When your staff believe that they are working towards a common purpose, rather than be-ing bullied into doing individual tasks for a purpose which has not been properly explained, their attitude will be more upbeat.

3. Repetition of intent or status—Keep reiterating corpo-rate messages or goals to staff. For instance, 'We are No. 1', 'Customer service comes first' or 'We provide unrivalled qual-ity'. The messages serve as important hooks on which to hang every single action during the working day.

> **4. Make your place of work a great place to work**—It is no coincidence that the companies which are the best places to work have the best business performances.

Effective delegation

There are three key issues when it comes to effective delegation:

1. MATCHING THE RIGHT PEOPLE TO THE TASK

Many examples of bad management simply come down to inadequate delegation. As a manager, you must make it your priority to know the strengths and weaknesses of your staff as well as the amount of work they undertake in any given week. This way you will be able to match the right challenge to the right person and neither underestimate nor overburden your staff.

Mind Maps can be very helpful in this respect, as you can Map the member of your team and catalogue their ability and experience. Return to your Mind Maps regularly, adding new skills learned or tasks mastered. You will then be able to gauge your staff's ability to cope with more responsibility and build up their skills at a rate where they enjoy the challenge but are not hopelessly out of their depth.

2. COMMUNICATING WHAT NEEDS TO BE DONE

All too often managers know the outcome they want, but fail to communicate this effectively to their staff. If, when the job is completed, the result is not as good as it could have been, the chances are it is because the brief was unclear.

Avoid this by giving clear instructions when you delegate and making yourself available for further questions when your team member gets going. Mind Maps are the perfect brief as they provide an overview of your vision for the task in question on a single page.

Using Mind Maps for team survival

Rikki Hunt is the former managing director of Burmah Oil and is currently the chairman of Fuel Force which turns over a billion pounds a year. He went on an expedition with a novice British team with the aim of determining the exact position of the Magnetic North Pole. Before the expedition, he used Mind Maps to plan his trip in terms of the kit he needed to take, but Mind Maps really came into their own when he was planning sharing very close living quarters in a small tent (5 ft × 6 ft) with four other people:

'When you are asleep in your bag and someone turns over, they can't unless you all do! It can go down to minus 50°C in the tent. Emotionally, it is very hard to feel positive, so Mind Mapping that out in advance and anticipating specific problems can help you. It is a very positive tool to help me get prepared. One of the things I did was to Mind Map how we should organize ourselves as a team. The organizers had said that we should have a rota, so one person cooks on Monday and a different person cooks on Tuesday. Someone collects the snow for water and another person puts up the tent. Using Mind Mapping, we established that we had someone in our tent who likes to cook. So rather than just cook on Monday, he cooked every night. We also had someone who didn't mind going out in the bad weather to collect the snow for cooking. So rather than have a rota, we created an environment that worked for everybody.'

3. TRUSTING YOUR STAFF TO DO A GOOD JOB

If you have delegated the task appropriately and communicated what you need accomplished, then you can be confident that the member of your team will perform the task to your satisfaction.

You need to trust your staff not only because it frees you up to do what you need to achieve, but also because it is important that your staff have ownership of what they do.

Employees who do not feel ownership of anything at work and who are denied responsibility are likely to feel dissatisfied and poorly motivated.

Rikki Hunt's story demonstrates beautifully how Mind Maps can assist teams in working out everyone's strengths and weaknesses, so that tasks can be delegated fairly and appropriately.

They can also help with advance team planning, particularly if, as in Rikki's example, immense challenge is actually synonymous with survival.

TEFCAS for praise and constructive criticism

Another extremely important role as a manager and leader is to give your staff feedback on what they do. This way they can learn from their successes and mistakes and grow from them. It is for this aspect of management that TEFCAS comes into its own (for detailed information on TEFCAS see Chapter 3). To recap, TEFCAS stands for:

- **T**rial
- **E**vent
- **F**eedback
- **C**heck
- **A**djust
- **S**uccess

1. PRAISE

Too many managers are quicker to criticize their staff than to praise, yet the importance of positive feedback where deserved cannot be more emphasized. Where it is earned, praise will motivate your team and give them the confidence to aim higher and achieve even greater things. Never underestimate the power of positive feedback. Even if your member of staff has made many mistakes, try to weave in some positive observations that they can latch on to and store in their experience bank as something they can develop and build on.

2. CONSTRUCTIVE CRITICISM

When you are managing a team, there will be times when mistakes have been made and need to be discussed. After all, it is almost certain that in order to get to the position you are in today, you will have experienced failure of one kind or another. Many people find it difficult to take criticism because they are worried it highlights them as having failed.

Failure can have a devastating effect on a person's confidence and sense of self-worth, especially if it might result in a humiliating job loss or demotion.

In general, fear of failure is more common than failure itself and this can be far more damaging to a business: it means that a company and its staff won't take risks. A company that is unable to take risks will never be cutting edge or a market leader. This is because risk-taking, albeit measured risk-taking, and the ability to learn from failure is part of every successful business's growth and evolution. This is what marks out the exceptional businessperson from the ordinary.

The power of persistence

According to Dr Adrian Atkinson, a business psychologist and managing director of Human Factors International, most entrepreneurs fail an average of five times before they are finally

---

> successful. Atkinson also observes that entrepreneurs regard
> failure as learning experiences which help them keep going.

Like the best entrepreneurs, you too should use your team's failures as an opportunity for learning. The TEFCAS success mechanism will help you and your team focus on what went wrong, why and what you can do to prevent the same happening again or to turn the situation into a success. This will ensure that criticism is constructive and not undermining.

TEFCAS IN ACTION

* Make sure that your team is familiar with the TEFCAS success mechanism and that you use it regularly in team meetings to analyze your results and performance as a group. The TEFCAS mechanism allows for failure, or error, as part of its formula to success so your team will soon get into the habit of analyzing their mistakes and interpreting what they have learned into their next success.

* When it comes to giving constructive criticism, sit down with your team or team member and have an open discussion of what happened and why. Draw a Mind Map of the situation to aid your discussion based on the six aspects of TEFCAS, namely:

1. TRIAL. What was the aim of the project or task and how did the team or person go about it?

2. EVENT. What was the outcome of the task or project in question?

3. FEEDBACK. What went well? What went wrong? What could have been done better? Should you have given your team or team member more help or advice?

4. CHECK. What do you think could be done to improve the situation? How can you ensure that the same mistakes aren't made again? What did work and what should be kept in place? What have you learned from the experience?

5. ADJUST. How can you go about implementing the necessary changes? As the team leader, do you need to give more direct input?

6. SUCCESS. What is the way forward? What are your new goals for the project? What will be the rewards for when it works next time?

* By looking at strengths as well as shortcomings of the person or team concerned, you will demonstrate that you are looking at the team or person as a whole and not simply picking up on the negatives in their performance. This will earn you respect and help you solicit the best from your staff in the future.

* If your team members feel supported the chances are they will be able to make the necessary adjustments to improve their performance.

Microsoft: strength from weakness

Microsoft is constantly praised as a success story in the business world. Bill Gates, Microsoft's chairman and chief software architect, loves innovation, is an inspirational leader and has built up an enviable corporate culture which often sees Microsoft scoring high in surveys dedicated to revealing the best and most productive workplaces around the world.

What has driven Microsoft's success over the years is an inherent ability to look at a piece of software through objective eyes and recognize its failings as well as its strengths. Bill Gates, addressing an audience in the US when launching

---

133

Microsoft's latest software innovations, referred to a past challenge which faced the company and how Microsoft dealt with it:

'If anything proves our willingness to listen to our customers and improve, it's the evolution of Word over the years. No doubt that first version was a little clunky, a little bit too much of a technologist's dream. We listened hard. People asked us to change it, and we drove it forward.'

For the world's richest man to accept and admit to flaws, as well as to attach so much importance to listening, shows why Gates is such an inspirational character

If you can teach your staff to overcome their fear of failure, they will be motivated to seize the initiative and manage themselves. Their positive ideas will interact synergetically, producing a creative hotbed of ideas. It may be that sometimes a potential solution turns out not to be so clever after all, but this is far more positive than being stuck in an endless cycle where nothing is ever challenged or changed. Remember:

SUCCESS IS OFTEN PRECEDED BY INITIAL FAILURE

And the vital ingredient you need to help achieve your goals is:

PERSISTENCE

MANAGING KNOWLEDGE

The way that knowledge is managed within a company is a powerful contributor to successful business performance. As a leader, it is your job not only to ensure that you have all possible relevant up-to-date facts and figures at your fingertips, but also to engender a culture of knowledge management throughout the company.

One of the main ways in which companies can differentiate themselves in today's overcrowded marketplace is through their specialist knowledge. A company which has the ability to predict market trends will clearly enjoy a competitive edge. And any company which has a strong tradition of expertise in a particular area is able to stay one step ahead.

Knowledge management can take place within a formal structure, such as regular meetings run by Mind Maps to assist in swapping and sharing information and ideas. Or it can be in a more informal scenario, such as comparing notes when meeting by the water cooler.

A primary goal of knowledge management is to accumulate and then disseminate this knowledge into your company culture so that it is accessible to everyone, regardless of where they are in the corporate hierarchy. Mind Maps are an excellent tool for keeping people up to date about the company and the marketplace in which it operates. With Mind Maps displayed around the workplace relating to areas such as customers, competitor companies and product developments, teams will constantly be aware of the bigger picture.

Designers and engineers at Boeing use Mind Maps to keep each other informed about each other's latest ideas and project developments. When they have new ideas or have completed something on their projects, they add this information to the shared Mind Map, to keep the other members of the team up to speed and to spark new ideas (*see also* 'No boredrooms at Boeing' p. 188).

A company which understands the importance of knowledge management and how it can impact on the bottom line, encourages everyone within the company to think more radiantly. Use Mind Maps to prompt and to mirror this radiant thinking.

Effective knowledge management

1. COMMITTING TO LEARNING

Invest in your own and your team's lifelong learning. Make sure that your highest priority is to introduce 'learning how to learn' training that incorporates Mind Mapping, creative thinking, memory, speed reading, study techniques and communication skills. These are the essential bases of all knowledge management. With these brain skills firmly in place, knowledge will be gained faster, comprehended more easily, remembered more completely and applied more appropriately. Without these skills, 80% of what is learned will be forgotten within 24 hours.

You and your working team should make sure that you scan regularly the media for information relevant to your workplace and that you record it all on Mind Maps. Together, you should apply your 'learning how to learn' knowledge to the continued assimilation of new skills, including languages, which will help benefit the business and give you and the team a deeper and broader basis from which to work. As a consequence, the team will become more involved and motivated, and will feel more valuable and more valued.

2. INVESTING IN THE TEAM KNOWLEDGE BANK

A team of people possesses an immense shared knowledge bank. If each team member has access to each other's million million brain cells and the incredible amount of knowledge stored therein, all this information could contribute towards making the company even more successful.

The best way to manage the information in your knowledge bank is to use computer Mind Maps. Computer Mind Maps such as 'Mind Genius' have the advantage of enabling you to macro- and micro-manage your knowledge. For more information see Chapter 7, 'Presentation Power'.

3. TAKE AN ACTIVE INTEREST

Encourage your staff to see their job as more than just a means to a pay cheque. Introduce them to clients, give them relevant reading matter, particularly Mind Maps, and ask for their opinions about the industry in which they work. If your team takes an active interest in the industry, some interesting and insightful perspectives are sure to arise. Arm them with the confidence to speak their minds and share their thoughts.

Motivating your team to become excellent knowledge managers

- Attend events with them.
- Share relevant information in Mind Map form.
- Encourage their interest in the industry in which you both work.
- Be full of enthusiasm for your industry and become one of its chief supporters. You can demonstrate your own enthusiasm by becoming involved with trade bodies and by speaking at forums and conferences.
- Be available to your team members as someone they can turn to for motivation and guidance about business matters.

MANAGING YOUR CUSTOMERS AND CLIENTS

A very important goal of your business is to satisfy customers in order that they will continue to trade with you. And this is tantamount to a definition of profitability. If profitability concerns itself purely and simply with making money, sooner or later the company will sink without trace. But if a business exists to provide a service to customers that those customers continue to want, it will survive.

Mind Maps are a way of organizing a business so that it can be customer-centric. The most talented customer-service personnel are those who forge good relationships with their customers to the extent that they may become friends. The close relationship developed should lead the customer to feeling a loyalty to your company and an interest in its continued success. This is a position which can only be mutually beneficial.

When you are managing a business, it is vital that you and your team have a clear picture in your mind of your client base. To achieve this, you need to begin by Mind Mapping your target clients (*see* the example opposite). A true picture of a client base is reliant on the quality and quantity of information and research that has been carried out. When building up a Mind Map picture from statistical research, the results are sometimes surprising, and always illuminating.

MIND MAPPING YOUR TARGET CUSTOMERS

1. Draw a sketch of your typical customer in the centre of your Mind Map so that you have a visual prompt. Think about your customers as if they are characters in a film or a book. You may even want to consider giving them names.

2. Draw main branches from your central image, sticking to one word per line, giving the basic information about your customers. These will be broad categories such as their gender, financial situation, lifestyle, priorities and values, age and interests.

3. On the sub-branches, you can flesh out your customers on the Mind Map, going into greater detail. Draw images throughout your Mind Map to really bring it to life. For instance, under 'finances', you may guess their salaries to be around £40,000 a year, and that they spend considerably on entertainment, holidays, clothing, beauty products and presents.

4. Once you have a rough Mind Map, share it with the team so you can develop the ideas together. And every time you have reason to

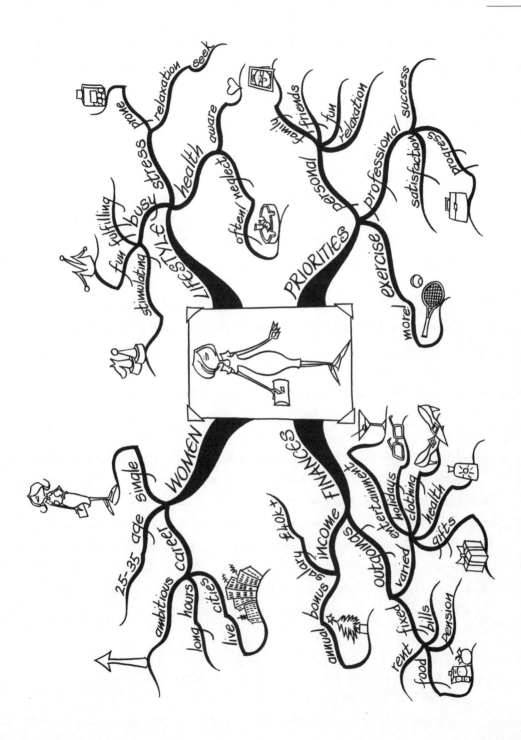

change slightly your view of your target client, so should you adjust your Mind Map.

Understanding your customers

Now you have a good idea of the type of person your target customers are, you will have a much better idea of how to approach them and talk to them when you do finally make contact.

Many business people dread meeting clients, seeing it at best as more of a chore than a pleasure. Yet meeting up with your customers is undoubtedly the best possible way of improving your mutual understanding of the business you work in. Managing your relationship with your customers is one of the most profitable investments of time and energy you will ever make.

Although you have a stereotypical image in your mind of your 'target customer', in reality, of course, everyone is different. However, they will all appreciate personal and focused attention. Remembering your customers' names and details about their lives always creates a favourable impression (for some hints on improving your memory, see the next section). Next, get into the habit of Mind Mapping new customers every time you meet up. This will be an ongoing Mind Map which reflects everything they have ever told you about themselves.

In the same way you Mind Mapped your target customers, start with their name and a brief physical description of your individual customer at the centre of the Mind Map—or, better still, a drawing of them. You can create a branch each for family, interests, profession, career history and holidays.

As you start to build up information about them, adding it to your Mind Map as you go, you will begin to know them like friends. Your Mind Map will be a colourful database, offering an instant update on exactly who your customers are. As a consequence you will:

• Be more confident with your customers, since you have been looking forward to seeing them;

- Be more attentive about what has been happening in their lives;
- Be more willing and able to meet your customers' needs, as you have found out what their actual needs are;
- Welcome them with open arms because you are interested in them and they are flattered by your interest;
- Find they want to do more business with you.

A GOOD MEMORY MAKES A LASTING IMPRESSION

1. REPETITION

When you are introduced to someone, repeat their name back to them. Notice anything unusual about the name. If it is a difficult name to pronounce, make sure you have the pronunciation absolutely correct. Use their name soon after meeting them, so it becomes real in your mind. If you are being introduced in a business environment, make sure you get their business card so you can see their name written down. Write the pronunciation down phonetically on the back of the business card if it is at all complicated.

You can also draw a quick Mind Map on the back of their business card with a rough sketch of their face at the centre and the curved branches as vital pieces of information which they have shared with you. This serves as a useful reminder if you need to telephone that person or if you meet them again. Names continually vex people, but it is well worth putting in the effort.

A good way to ensure that people remember your name is to incorporate it into your conversation by using direct instead of reported speech. So instead of saying 'My boss asked me if I wanted to go to that conference' say 'My boss said to me, "Tony, would you like to go that conference?" ' This helps your name to gel in other people's minds and makes the conversation more interesting and alive.

2. TAKING AN INTEREST

If you take more of an interest in your surroundings, it will be harder for you to forget the details. If you go on holiday, read guidebooks about the place you are visiting. There might be an interesting story behind the name of the town that cements the place-name in your memory.

Similarly, when you meet people, take an interest in them. Ask them questions about themselves, their families and where they live. If you are at a business function, it is likely that you will know some of the same people. This will help to flesh out the Mind Map that you prepare for that person. After you have met someone whom you want to make a point of remembering, mentally review that person once a day over the next seven days. Use your imagination to make the details that you have learnt about that person stick in your mind.

3. VISUALIZATION

When you have just met someone and have spoken to them about their interests, use your imagination to visualize them doing the things they love most. For instance, if they are into skiing, imagine them whizzing down the snowy slopes on a bright sunny day. If they live in the country, imagine their house, surrounded by green fields. Not only does this make the conversation more interesting for your brain, the association with a particular image, location or sensation will help to entrench that person in your memory.

4. PAY ATTENTION

Follow up taking an interest with paying attention. It is bad manners to ask someone a question and then give them only half of your attention while your gaze wanders around the room, searching for a preferable conversation partner. Be prepared to be surprised by the people who you meet, rather than seeing networking as a chore.

5. MAKE MEMORY YOUR HOBBY

If you make memory your hobby, you will relish the challenge and see it as a fun game rather than an impossible task. Encourage your colleagues to do the same if you are at a business function together. Test each other on people's names and what they do within the company. See if you can remember interesting facts about them (making sure that you add them to your Mind Maps when you are back in your office). This will have significant long-term effects on your business; before long you will stride confidently into any situation, armed with knowledge about the people you are meeting.

Knowledge is power in any business situation. And what is more, your clients, customers and associates will be flattered that you have taken the trouble to remember so much about them. Not only will they make more of an effort with you and your team by way of reciprocating the favour, they will also be much more likely to do business with you as opposed to with your competitors.

DEALING WITH THE COMPETITION

Good management includes being aware of the competition, but not becoming obsessed by it. It is crucial to make sure you continue to attract the largest possible proportion of the potential customers out there. To do this you must make sure that whatever it is you are offering always has an edge on your rival's product.

For this, it is an invaluable exercise to Mind Map the competitor companies. For instance, if you run a hairdressing salon and another salon opens up on the same street, you will need to protect your customer base by finding out exactly what the new salon is offering.

MIND MAPPING THE COMPETITION

Before you start Mind Mapping your competition, you will need to research that competition, including details of the company's structure, what they offering and how much they charge:

1. Draw a Mind Map with the competitor company at the centre.

2. On your main branches, include that company's management and staff, their customers and the location. You should also add strengths and weaknesses as well as any of the new salon's unique selling points.

3. On the sub-branches, you need to go into greater detail. Not only will this give you a clearer idea of the competition, but it will also help you look at your own business in a new light. At this stage you should examine the competition's unique selling points more closely. It may be that you can easily match or outperform them.

See where your own company's Mind Map overlaps with that of the competition. This will be graphic representation of where you are ahead of the game and where you have some ground to make up. From this point you can Mind Map a plan of action.

Understanding customer behaviour

In any business, you are guaranteed repeat orders from your customers if you can understand the simple truths about who they are and what they want.

Being proactive instead of reactive pays dividends in business. This is why it is such a valuable exercise to monitor continuously your customers' behaviour with Mind Maps. This enables you to identify factors such as the competition, consumer trends and changes in the supply and demand chain—and how they may be encroaching on your business.

It will also give you insight into patterns of consumption for your particular product or service. It does not matter whether your business is large or small, the benefits of taking the time and trouble to reflect on what you are doing and how it fits into the bigger picture is vital to business success.

The TEFCAS success mechanism can come into play here (*see*

pp. 51–5). Ask your customers for feedback so you can check and adjust your operation in order to maintain your success.

Managing customer loyalty

As most markets are flooded with businesses, yours has to stand out from the crowd. An increasingly popular way in which businesses are retaining their customers is through customer relationship marketing schemes (CRM).

CRM success at Tesco

The supermarket chain Tesco is frequently cited as an example of a company that successfully attracts and maintains customer loyalty. It keeps close to its customers with its main customer relationship marketing (CRM) scheme, Clubcard.

Through its Clubcard scheme, Tesco collects valuable information about its customers. That way, it is able to send promotional offers to them, informed by their shopping habits. Its mailings can target anyone who shops at Tesco, from wine lovers to penny-conscious parents. The CRM programme has contributed significantly to the store's success—in 2003, Tesco announced an increase in annual profits of £1.3 billion and a rise in operating profits of 7%.

Tesco has also changed the perception of the brand from cheap and cheerful to friendly and 'on the customer's side'. This has allowed the company to experiment with other methods of winning customer loyalty such as Tesco.com—one of the UK's most-widely used groceries website—and the Tesco Baby and Toddler Club through which parents can swap information in chatrooms run by Tesco's online partner, www.ivillage.co.uk.

Using a Mind Map, think of ways in which your business can develop its relationship with customers using CRM techniques.

MIND MAPPING CRM TECHNIQUES

1. Draw a satisfied customer at the heart of your Mind Map.

2. Draw main branches from your central image which incorporate CRM tools such as 'loyalty schemes', 'offers', 'vouchers', 'previews', 'special clubs', 'internet chatrooms' and 'events'.

3. Draw sub-branches, investigating in more detail the CRM tools available to you.

4. Next, using colour, prioritize each CRM tool in terms of your customers, indicating which ones would mean the most to them. For instance, if your customers are value-conscious, vouchers may be a good way of winning their loyalty. If most of your customers are online, communicating with them via chatrooms or by making online offers might be a more efficient way of grabbing their attention.

5. Use your Mind Map as a springboard for discussion among your team about how to improve your relationship with your customers.

Improving performance with customer consultation

If your company has been underperforming, then your first step on the road to recovery is to Mind Map the company's true position. You will get the best results if you involve all your team members as well as all your customers in this process.

MIND MAPPING CUSTOMER FEEDBACK

Ask everyone who works for the company to name three things they love and three things they dislike about the company. Then ask everyone who is in contact with your customers to ask them for the same.

Do not feel embarrassed about being so direct with your customers; they will appreciate your willingness to improve and—as this exercise will ultimately benefit them—they will be happy to co-operate.

Collate all the answers and then use them to prepare a mega-Mind Map:

1.   Put your company as the central image of the Mind Map.

2.   Draw main branches from your central image, representing recurrent themes in your feedback. These may include areas such as 'customer service', 'fulfilment' and 'communication'.

3.   Explore a plan of action through creating sub-branches looking clearly at the areas that need the most attention.

This Map will give you a clear sense of direction in how to progress in a customer-centric manner. The messages of this Mind Map need to be communicated throughout the organization. It may be helpful to feedback the results to your customers as well, where possible outlining how you plan to act on the results.

MANAGING YOUR BUSINESS ENVIRONMENT

A less appreciated but nevertheless important aspect of leadership is that of ensuring that your team is given the optimum environmental conditions for fulfilling their roles.

Studies have shown that the office environment has a profound effect on the health, mood, attitude and energy of those working in that environment.

This, in turn, is reflected in the creativity, productivity and success of the team.

An ideal environment is one that stimulates the senses and keeps the brain alert and active, making the sort of place you would like to be in anyway. However, if a workplace has none of these characteristics, then team members will enter it with reluctance.

A manager should be aware of the crucial importance of the office environment and strive to make it as welcoming and stimulating as possible.

Making brain room

Many businesses have realized the importance of the office environment. The Finnish company Digital Equipment designed an entire office using Mind Maps. They created an environment expressly to promote brain stimulation and body health.

Salen, the Swedish shipping group, used Mind Maps to design a 'brain room', to stimulate and relax the mind. They achieved this with a careful use of colour and art, Mind Maps and challenging games, such as chess and Go.

WH Smith are developing a 'brain-friendly' HQ in order to help nurture and promote creativity. To do this they will looking at the use of:

- Light
- Art
- Plants
- Textures
- Colours
- Mind Map tools

A number of very senior and professional organizations are being led to the conclusion by their Mind Maps that their offices need to be more like kindergartens. This is based on the perhaps startling revelation that people work best when they play. As Hippocrates said, 'You will never see anything as serious as a child at play.'

In the appropriate working environment, the imagination is freed up, creativity enhanced and, just as we are less prone to becoming tired when at play, energy and staying power is increased.

Changing and optimizing the business environment is the perfect opportunity for Mind Mapping with the whole team. Each team member can make suggestions as to improvements and they can be added to a Mind Map and discussed together.

As with any makeover, this does not have to be an expensive initiative—all it takes is a little flexibility and a willingness to listen. And there is the advantage that this is bound to boost morale and to demonstrate the value of working as a team.

GOOD LEADERSHIP GETS RESULTS

The best managers are the ones who know how to channel the strengths of the people they lead into ever-greater successes. They support their staff through their mistakes and their weaknesses, and use them as opportunities for learning and future success.

Anyone aspiring to be a good business leader should make the following qualities an integral part of their approach:

* **Knowledge**—Good leaders make knowledge of their company, staff, customers and clients a priority. They always seek to improve themselves, to build up their own skills base and to share their experience with their teams.

❋ **Trust**—Good leaders put their trust in their teams. They know their staff are good—after all, they hired them.

❋ **Praise**—Good leaders give praise when a job is well done. And they always give credit where credit is due, not claiming the praise for themselves.

❋ **Failure-friendly**—Good leaders see failure as an opportunity to learn rather than for promoting a culture of blame and shame. They employ the TEFCAS success mechanism, understanding that failure is an essential ingredient for success.

❋ **Encouragement**—Modern leaders have moved on from an aggressive management style. Instead, they encourage creativity, growth, learning, responsibility and teamwork.

❋ **Listening**—Good leaders do more listening than talking because they are always eager to learn.

At all times you should lead your team by example and demonstrate the vision, commitment and integrity that you expect from your staff.

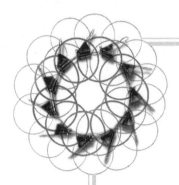

6

Beat the
Bullies

There are bullies in all walks of life and the workplace is no exception. In reality, it is the bully who has the problem, lacks the confidence and social skills to interact with others in a responsible and thoughtful way. But this fact does not prevent their attentions blighting the lives of others. In this chapter, we take a look at bullying at work and investigate how Mind Maps can be used to help deal with it.

Bullying can manifest in numerous ways and has been defined as behaviour which hurts or causes distress by taking advantage of the vulnerability of the victim. All forms of bullying can lie on a continuum ranging from mild to severe—physical abuse can range from pinching and shoving into people to serious assault; verbal abuse may be unwanted teasing or it might be threats, malicious gossip and spreading damaging rumours; interfering with another's possessions is also a form of bullying. Lastly, sexual harassment of any sort is also a form of bullying, whether in the form of inappropriate comments or actions.

As we have seen, a healthy work environment is one where the team members are able to express their talents to the full in a positive environment. Although most workplaces can sometimes be the source of stressful situations, beyond this, the causing of intentional upset to any degree is quite unacceptable on a personal level, as well as being counterproductive for the team as a whole. Bullying is one of the great destroyers in businesses. It creates an atmosphere of oppression, depression and fear, and all these are guaranteed to reduce the effectiveness of individuals and organizations. With this in mind, it is in the interests of leaders and team members alike to address the issue of bullying.

The big friendly giant

Some 15 years ago, I was doing some work with the retail chain Littlewoods. One of the senior managers was a big man, 6' 4" and physically very strong, with a booming voice that made the walls shake as he spoke.

Some members of staff had told me that he was a bully, always imposing himself on them and bossing them around. They said they were terrified of him.

In conversation with him, while Mind Mapping his functions at the company, I asked him to add to the Mind Map what his perceptions were of what the members of his team thought of him. The words he used were along the lines of 'kind', 'visionary' and 'supportive'. When I told him that there were those who thought him a bully, his face fell in sorrow and bewilderment.

Quite simply, he hadn't realized that a combination of his imposing physical presence, together with his enthusiasm and passion for his job, came over to others as arrogance and bullying.

Subsequently, I brought both sides together and we compared their Mind Maps of this person. Surprisingly, they came very close to matching, and the difficulty was purely one of interpretation. The staff realized that in fact he was a wonderful boss, and in turn he learned that in future he must make sure that he projects himself unambiguously.

Clearly, bullies do exist in the workplace and, if the strategies outlined here do not resolve the situation, then action must be taken through the appropriate channels. However, there are times when bullying is a state of mind, either resulting from a misperception of a situation, or deriving from internal negative self-talk (*see* pp. 169–70).

As the story demonstrates, it is important to be aware that bullying behaviour can be unintentional—in fact, quite the opposite was intended in this case. The problem is frequently one of perception and a lack of clear communication. By regularly Mind Mapping within a team, any actual problems can be picked up on and dealt with, while misconceptions can be stamped out in their early stages before they take hold and become blown out of proportion. If you are in doubt about whether there are crossed wires, you should approach the person involved and explore this possibility.

BULLYING IN THE WORKPLACE

If you have ever heard yourself, or any of your friends and family, saying any of the following, it may be that you have been the subject of bullying at work:

'I'm never given any credit for the things I've done.'
'I hate my boss!'
'I feel like I'm constantly being criticized.'
'They make me feel like I'm nothing.'
'She's such a control freak.'
'I don't trust my boss at all. All he's interested in is making himself look good to his superiors.'
'I don't know what's wrong with me or what I'm doing wrong, but I always seem to be under attack about something.'

Bullies contaminate the atmosphere in any workplace, making everyone on the team feel tense and intimidated. Bullies hamper energy and productivity.

Their mood conquers everything and is characterized by inconsistency: they may be in a brilliant mood one day, meaning that the team relaxes and becomes a hotbed of creativity . . . until the next day when the bully is back to his old tricks. And let's be clear about one thing here: when I say 'his old tricks', in fact bullies in the workplace can just as easily be male or female.

Spite and sabotage

Alan was highly regarded by other members of the team for his technical know-how and worked well with his colleagues. However, there were three troublemakers in the team who were contractors and any attempt at gaining cooperation from them was simply ignored or dealt with by an 'I'm too busy' response. Gradually there was a build-up of 'hostility' towards Alan who they resented for his ability and reliability, as well as his willingness to work late at night.

Soon, misleading messages involving fabricated requests to contact other members of staff were put on Alan's desk. Spiteful, vexatious and malicious rumours were seeded in the office by the three. Deliberate sabotage of work that Alan had been involved in took place. Eventually, the other members of the team felt so intimidated by the three, that they kept away from any social exchanges with Alan. Alan eventually found the working conditions so intolerable that he left.

Bullies block creativity and imagination, since targets of bullying become increasingly fixated on the bully's behaviour rather than their own ideas or creative thoughts. Eventually, targets of bullying withdraw into themselves and find it hard to focus on the bigger picture, let alone contribute to it. (I recommend you visit **www.bullyonline.org** for more on how to recognize bullies and their behaviour and also read my two books, *The Power of Social Intelligence* and *The Power of Spiritual Intelligence*.)

FROM PLAYGROUND TO WORKPLACE

As a child, you were familiar with the school bully. Terrorizing and violent, the bully made it clear that the school playground was his territory. Anyone who crossed his path would soon understand who was in charge.

The bully at work is no different. She is still an insecure child and behaves in an immature fashion, ganging up on some colleagues, alienating others. And like an attention-seeking child, she feels the need to dominate any situation.

Bullies find it impossible to take responsibility for their own behaviour. In the event of something going wrong, they are the first to point the finger of blame rather than accept responsibility themselves. They see nothing wrong with this behaviour, and will judge it as their right to behave in such a fashion.

THE ROOTS OF WORKPLACE BULLYING

With the longest working hours in Europe, the UK is particularly susceptible to bullying in the workplace. The TUC estimates that 4 million people regularly work over 48 hours every week, which means the average employee takes on approximately £5,000 of unpaid labour every year.

When you take into account the fact that managers have often been promoted to their positions without any prior managerial experience or training, you then have the sort of pressured environment from which bullies emerge.

As they are insecure in their new roles, many of these inexperienced managers make an effort to prove themselves by coming across as aggressive or tough. This turns them into bullies rather than managers, with potentially devastating effects on their staff and the businesses which they are supposed to be managing.

THE COST OF BULLYING

If you work in a human-resources department, you need to understand just how devastating bullying can be. From your personal knowledge of bullying in the workplace, create Mind Maps of its macro- and micro-consequences.

THE IMPACT OF BULLYING ON ORGANIZATIONS

Start by Mind Mapping how a culture of bullying can affect your company as a whole, looking at it from both an insider's and outsider's perspective.

1. For your central image, draw a cartoon image of a bully.

2. The words touching your main branches could be 'absenteeism', 'morale', 'image' and 'customers'. Explore any other theme that is appropriate to your industry or workplace.

3. From your main branches, draw sub-branches exploring each issue in turn. For instance, under 'absenteeism' might come 'stress' and 'productivity'; under 'image', take into account that 'shareholders' and 'investors' will think twice about whether they want to be involved with an organization which has a reputation for bullying its workforce.

4. Use colours and pictures throughout to make the messages of your Mind Map clear. This is an important Mind Map for you to learn and absorb, so spending the time on making it memorable will pay dividends.

5. Share the Mind Map with the rest of your team so that everyone in the organization is clear about the destructive nature of bullying.

Now draw a second Mind Map which looks at bullying from the target's point of view.

THE IMPACT OF BULLYING ON INDIVIDUALS

1. For the centre of this Mind Map draw an image or use a photo of someone who has been bullied. They might appear angry, depressed or defeated.

2. Your main branches might include words such as 'anger', 'escapism', 'relationships' and 'stress'.

3. Explore the issues on your main branches by extending out into sub-branches. Stress-related conditions as a direct consequence of bullying include:

- Depression
- Post-traumatic stress disorder
- Chronic fatigue syndrome (ME)
- Alopecia
- Sleeplessness
- Skin conditions

Under relationships, explore what bullying is responsible for in terms of breaking up relationships and disrupting family life. Under 'fear', bear in mind that even strong personalities have been devastated by bullying and have turned into frightened and confused shadows of their former selves. Possessed by guilt, they feel in some way that it is their fault they are bullied; they become embarrassed and ashamed of what they perceive to be their own shortcomings.

4. Again, ensure that everyone in the company sees this Mind Map so they can become aware of the pernicious effects of bullying.

Armed with these two Mind Maps you will have made a step forward in beginning to stamp out bullying in the organization.

> ### How doctors are at risk
>
> The medical profession is a particular target for bullying. A random sample of 1,000 doctors working in different capacities for the National Health Service were questioned by the British Medical Association News Review about bullying in the workplace. The response was staggering. One in three staff reported that they had been bullied over the past year. It is the same story in the USA where studies have shown that medical students suffer from mistreatment or bullying during their training period.

Those who can do, those who can't bully

This headline was aptly coined for the 'Bullying at Work' page of **www.bullyonline.org**—the web site of the UK National Workplace Bullying Advice Line. If you are, or ever have been, bullied at work, you may take some comfort from the following statistic: in at least 95% of the cases of bullying reported to the UK National Workplace Bullying Advice Line, the person had been picked on *because they are good at their job and popular with people.*

This is backed up by research by the Workplace Bullying and Trauma Institute (**www.bullyinginstitute.org**) which aims to help individuals and organizations in the US and Canada. In its 2003 report on abusive workplaces, the top five reasons why targets are subjected to bullying were:

1. I remained independent, refused to be controlled or subservient (70%);

2. My competence and reputation were threatening (67%);

3. The bully's personality (59%);

4. My being liked by co-workers and customers (47%);

5. In retaliation for my reporting unethical or illegal conduct; whistle-blowing (38%).

This shows clearly that a bully is weak, insecure, confused and irresponsible. Meanwhile, a bully's targets are more likely to be professional, responsible and popular.

UNDERSTANDING THE BULLY

In order to understand how to counter bullying in the workplace, it is helpful to profile the bully's personality by Mind Mapping it. This will enable you to remind yourself at a glance the reasons why this person is a bully. Whether it is you who are the subject of the bullying or if you are trying to resolve such issues amongst your team, as with the acquisition of knowledge in other contexts, this is an empowering process.

MIND MAPPING THE BULLY

1. Draw a picture of the bully at the centre of your Mind Map and write 'bully' in big letters next to it.

2. Along the main branches, write words which describe the bully. You may want to consider words such as 'jealous', 'hurtful', 'insecure', 'unhappy', 'violent' and 'irresponsible'. There is no limit on the number of words you can choose to use.

3. Next, using sub-branches, explore examples of when he has behaved in ways which match the adjectives on the main branches. For instance, is the bully manipulative in the sense of using mind games? Does the bully have favourites one week who are dropped like a hot brick the

next? Or is the bully controlling in the sense of being a control freak who has to have the last say on everything?

4.   If there is more than one person on the team who is undergoing a similar experience with the bully, include their comments in your Mind Map. Use a different colour to represent each voice as their experiences could be subtly different.

5.   Add to the Mind Map any new examples of the bully's behaviour. Simply by keeping a log of the behaviour on your Mind Map will make you feel empowered and in control of the situation. You will also start to notice patterns in the bullying which will help you and your team to recognize and eventually to anticipate the offensive behaviour.

CHOOSING YOUR TACTICS

Once you have finished work on your Mind Map, you have a range of choices open to you. These are contained, together with an analysis of the bully's personality, in the colour Mind Map 'Beat the bully'. Courses of action open include:

Understand

At first, try to understand rather than be understood. All human beings seek to be understood and this is a feeling you can connect with. Try and satisfy the bully's basic human desire to be understood. Remember, the bully is fundamentally insecure. It is likely that behind the façade of this aggressive immature behaviour is a lonely person desperately seeking love and approval. It is not your role to provide this—you are at your place of work to earn a living—but a little empathy and forgiveness can be of help.

Avoid provocation

Although the bully has got under your skin, avoid being provoked into criticizing yourself or taking things out on your friends, family and colleagues. By the same token, don't take what might seem an easy route and escape into comfort eating or the excess consumption of alcohol, cigarettes and other drugs. The best way to manage yourself when you are suffering the attentions of a bully is to take pride and boost your self-esteem by *not* reacting in a negative way. In nature, it is the weak that get turned upon, and so by behaving as a victim you would become even more of a target. At the same time, it is as well to read the signs and learn to avoid putting yourself in the firing line. Don't think this shows weakness on your part. It simply shows that you are not prepared to play the bully's game. (*See* 'Fighting back', p. 168.)

Manage your anger

It is not surprising that a bully can make you feel incandescent with rage. This may be because the bully has:

- Insulted you;
- Called into question your professional integrity;
- Taken the credit for your creative idea;
- Blamed you for something going wrong that was not your fault.

But if you are suffering from the attentions of a bully, the more adversely you react, the more likely the bully is to repeat the behaviour. If, on the other hand, you are able to avoid provocation and control your anger, walking away from situations with your dignity and humour intact, the bully will not have received the gratification that was craved. Although in the very short term this may lead to an escalation in attempts at bullying, this is soon likely to subside. The more you can shrug it off, the less of a target you will become, with the bully being more intimidated by your newfound self-assurance.

THE POWER OF VISUALIZATION

Bear in mind that a Mind Map is a graphic, and as such is a powerful visualization tool, because it combines many interlinked images in one master image.

So, in dealing with a bully, always use a Mind Map as your ultimate visualization of both the strategy and tactics you will use in changing the bully's behaviour to your (mutual) advantage.

1. Spend a few minutes imagining yourself in a typical bullying situation. Use the Mind Maps you have drawn to prompt a typical situation.

2. Visualize the situation right down to the very last detail. But, this time, imagine your reaction to one of the bully's usual jibes. You are calm and collected.

3. Then you return to your work with grace and decorum, seemingly untouched by his cruel comments.

Suppose the bully is always telling you that your work isn't up to scratch, even though you put an enormous amount of time and effort into your work and go above and beyond the call of duty. Your normal reaction to being criticized is to burst into tears and cry on a colleague's shoulder. You then commence a moan-a-thon which continues after work over a few drinks. You return home, the worse for wear, and after a fitful night's sleep, are back in the office still feeling raw from the anger that consumed you the day before.

But if you have used the visualization process every day for a week, the barbed comments won't stick quite so readily. Next time, you won't spontaneously burst into tears and drown your sorrows. You will simply observe that the bully is trying to be hurtful. By way of response, be faultlessly polite in your dealings with this person, during and after the attack, and when the bully has finished, return to work as if nothing noteworthy has happened. Others will take their lead from you and soon the bully will back off, realizing it is a losing battle.

The bully might even see that, in a workplace full of such kind, polite and well-mannered people, there is simply no place for aggression and rudeness.

Confront

One course of action is to confront the bully, using your Mind Map to explain the situation and suggest resolutions. While this may not always be successful—some bully's problems are deep-seated—as long as you feel sure of your ground, you have nothing to lose in confronting the bully and everything to gain.

Some bullies are unaware of the hurtful effects their comments and actions can have (*see* 'The big friendly giant', p. 154). However, the fact that you are using a Mind Map shows that you intend to change this situation and demonstrates your strength and will to resolve the situation.

It takes guts to stand up to a bully. You will not only gain the respect of your peers and the bully, you will also increase your own self-respect. Your focused approach and straight-talking might steer the bully towards a more congenial way of working. If the problem continues and you have to take it further, it is important that you have tried to resolve the situation in a responsible and mature manner.

Seek advice

Seek out advice wherever possible. Bullying is such a widespread problem that many people have experience of it in one form or another. It may be that you are able to talk about it outside work with friends or family. Your Mind Map will be a useful and vivid record to share with them. Alternatively, perhaps there is a colleague at your place of work who is able to handle the bully in a particularly effective manner. If so, seek out that person and ask them about their tactics. It is preferable to keep such consultations as informal and low key as possible, only speaking with those whose discretion you can trust.

In addition, there are online organizations who have much experience in this field who are able to provide sound advice (*see* p. 160).

Ultimately, there will be occasions where bullying is so remorseless that further action might need to be considered, in terms of consulting with team leaders, personnel managers or union representatives. This is not a decision to be taken lightly, but if you have conducted yourself as suggested here, keeping a truthful Mind Map of everything that has happened, your self-respect will be enhanced, as will the admiration of your friends and colleagues.

Remain positive

After working with bullies for any length of time, your confidence may be so battered that you begin to believe the negative and abusive remarks that have been directed against you.

The advice from Janine, a former target of bullying in the workplace, is: 'I know it is hard, but try to remain positive and don't sink, because if you do, the bully has won yet again.'

You will be able to draw inner strength and pride from the fact that you do not let the bully's problems upset you or disrupt your life. You understand where the bully is coming from, you will do whatever seems necessary to alleviate the situation, but, in the meantime, you remain calm, smiling and happy, secure in yourself.

DISAPPOINTMENT IN THE WORKPLACE

When you have been on the receiving end of bullying, sometimes it is possible to become oversensitive to any adverse comment or reaction at work. It is important to keep a watch out for this and see situations from other people's perspectives.

The worst thing you can do when a bully has caused you genuine disappointment is to become defensive. However hard it may be, swallow down your instinct to shout in your defence. Wait till a time when things are calmer and then ask your boss to make his point of view clear to you. Perhaps he will be impressed by your ability to review your work and may think twice about taking such an aggressive stance towards you in the future.

Incorporate any comments he makes into a Mind Map so that he knows that you are serious about wanting to improve the quality of your work.

Keeping things in perspective

Imagine that, thanks to Mind Maps, you are brimming over with creative ideas and not afraid to take risks. But when you stride confidently into your boss's office and present your latest Mind Mapped idea with conviction, she doesn't show any enthusiasm for the idea and seems determined to bring you down a peg or two. How do you react to such disappointment while maintaining the harmony in the workplace? It may be that she was just using the situation to bully you and put you down, but equally it might be there were other reasons she was not enthused. Instead of taking matters too much to heart, keep these points in mind:

1. Timing is everything—Pick your moments carefully at work. If your boss has been in a long meeting all day and you pounce before she's had a chance to get a glass of water and look at the mail, then she is not likely to be in the most receptive mood to engage with you and your idea.

2. Always be prepared to improve—If you accept that an idea can always be improved upon, then if you face a situation where a boss says he hates an idea you came up with, you can ask him about his specific objections. He may like one part of your idea but not its entirety. Perhaps he wants to add to it and take it in a slightly different direction. Be prepared to compromise and talk through your idea rather than going in with a fixed attitude and being unwilling to be flexible and receptive to his input.

3. Let go—If your boss really doesn't like your idea, be prepared to let it go. It will only cause you more grief and tension in the long run if you don't. Instead, re-channel your energy on something else and see if you get a more positive response.

Fighting back

We live in a culture where fighting back is portrayed as the heroic thing to do. Endless films, books and TV series focus on men and women defending their honour by violent means. A common instinct to being bullied at work is to want to fight back. But so few people can fight back effectively and reach a satisfactory conclusion. More often, fighting back compounds a situation and both parties end up increasing each other's suffering.

Fighting back is perceived as the only other option to being walked all over. But often the best tactic is to walk away from someone whose mood is destructive and aggressive. Just like children who often need time to themselves to absorb something and learn from it, bullies also need that space. Walking away is not the same as being a pushover—giving in and accepting what the bully is saying—it is merely a refusal to become involved in someone else's negative mind games.

Armed with your Mind Maps you are able to reflect clearly on your own worth and on your actions. If you can honestly tell yourself that you have done your best and acted with integrity, then the poisoned barbs of others can just bounce off you.

The way of harmony

Training in a martial art such as aikido will give you the mental strength to be able to handle conflict in an enlightened way. Such training enables you to focus and be aware of the specifics of a situation, turning the dynamics of that situation to positive use, while shielding you from any negative actions and influences. Contrary to many long-held myths, the martial arts, and specifically aikido, are about finding a peaceful solution rather than a violent one. However inharmonious a situation may seem at first, a peaceful solution is always within your reach.

BEATING THE BULLY INSIDE YOUR HEAD

With the rise in awareness of bullying in the workplace, it has become clear that virtually all the discussions, articles and books on the subject centre on the assumption that bullying is perpetrated by one person on another. In fact, nothing could be farther from the truth.

By far the greatest number of bullies exist inside our heads rather than outside our bodies. Bullying in your head is the 'monkey on your shoulder', your negative-thinking pattern.

Modern UK and European culture focuses on finding faults and correcting mistakes, so unwittingly it focuses predominantly on the negative. And because the brain takes as its guide or vision whatever it is focused on, so people become habituated to focus on their mistakes, faults and weaknesses. As a result, the average person's 'self-talk' is weighted by about 15–1 in favour of negative thoughts and this has a cumulative effect of negative reinforcement, each negative idea laying down a new negative brain-cell pathway. It is the Big Bully within. The chances are that there is a bully inside you, who berates and abuses you with phases such as:

- 'I can't do it';
- 'I'm no good';

- 'I'm stupid';
- 'Things never go right for me';
- 'I'm a failure';
- 'I don't have the energy'.

But these comments are no more true than those coming from an outside bully. Again, they are self-destructive manifestations of inner feelings of insecurity, lack of confidence and self-esteem. On the face of it, it may appear that such self-deprecations are harmless, providing an easy get-out from situations and challenges you don't want to meet full on. In fact, they are very damaging and can lead to a downward spiral of fear, negativity, disappointment and self-disgust. In this way, your initial lack of confidence and self-esteem is compounded.

But life is for living, not for escaping. By putting the inner bully in its place, you will be free to get on with interacting vibrantly with life. At one level, not every challenge you meet will result in success, but at another level, if you face each challenge positively, honestly and to the best of your ability, you are a success. And as a result you will be happier, more respectful and respected.

TRAPPING THE BULLY WITHIN

1.   Draw a picture at the centre of your Mind Map of how you think your internal bully might look.

2.   Make main branches for all the negative thoughts you have, then draw sub-branches for how these make you feel, and how they might effect how you behave.

3.   When you have done this, make another Mind Map showing how each one of those can be transformed into a positive.

At the end of it all, sit back and laugh at the absurd theatre of it all and feel free. Push the monkey off your shoulder and liberate the unfettered positive creative force within.

PUTTING BULLYING IN ITS PLACE

Bullying at work is something that all businesses—and everyone who works in them—can do without, but sometimes have to cope with. All bullies seek out the weak and vulnerable, so the best approach to combat all forms of bullying (internal and external), is to empower oneself. As we have learnt elsewhere in this book, knowledge is power. By using Mind Maps we can:

- Understand the effect of bullying on individuals and organizations;
- Get inside the mind of the workplace bully;
- Learn to remain positive—after all, you are not the one with the problem;
- Beat the bully inside your own head.

When you are free of the attentions of any oppressive behaviour, from inside or out, you will be able to concentrate better on performing in the workplace in an optimum fashion, demonstrating to all your mastery of your skills and knowledge.

In the next chapter, we see how Mind Maps enable you to communicate your knowledge by giving vivid, memorable and informative presentations.

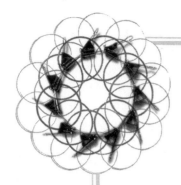

7

Presentation
Power

PRESENT IMPERFECT

I t is the early 1960s and a young university lecturer is lecturing first-year psychology students on the power of memory.

Just like countless lecturers before him, he prepares his presentation with a few pages of notes made up of linear sentences. Announcing his subject, he says, 'Today, the topic is memory.' He stands behind the podium at the front of the lecture hall and starts to read, expecting his diligent students to take 'proper notes', just as he did when he was in their shoes.

He presents information specifically about the requirements for memory to work. There are two main elements: imagination—incorporating images and sensual feedback—and associations or connections. As well as these two main elements, he says, memory works more efficiently when things stand out. Here, the lecturer remembers that very day over 40 years ago:

> '*As I droned monotonously on, going slowly enough so that the students could copy my words, I realized that I was boring myself to distraction. As I looked at the drooping shoulders, heavy heads and clenched hands as they tried to scribble my rubbish, I realized that I wasn't doing much for my students either.*

'In addition, although I was telling them that in order to remember something, it has to have images, associations and things that stand out, I was lecturing in a monotone voice, asking them to write page upon page of rigid single-colour notes, with no images, associations or anything that stood out. In other words, I was presenting to them the entire essence of memory in a manner that could have been designed to make them forget everything I said.'

That lecturer was me, and that lecture with the ironic contrast between subject matter and presentation came like a thunderbolt from the skies. Looking back on it, that lecture represented a watershed in how I presented information.

It became clear that I needed to convey information in a way that would assist the audience in understanding and remembering it. I needed to impart information in a form that was easily digested by the human brain—not in linear lumps, which would remain unabsorbed. I realized that from now on my lectures should no longer use just sentences, but also include key words and images, alongside connections and associations, as well as elements such as colour, shape and size to help significant points stand out.

It was also clear that this insight should apply not only to my presentations as a verbal speaker, but also to the presentation of my own thoughts on paper. It was as relevant to me in a personal sense as much as it was to the use of a blackboard, an overhead projector or a whiteboard.

So I went back to the drawing board—started with a 'blank slate', an imaginary white page—and asked myself two simple questions.

NEW WAYS WITH NOTE-TAKING

Q: What do I need, on this note page, to help trigger my imagination?

A: _____

Q: What do I need on this note page to help me associate those things that have triggered my imagination?

A: _____

The answers to the first question included:

- Images,
- Colours,
- Codes,
- Key image words,
- Symbols,
- Visual rhythms.

The answers to the second question included:

- Lines,
- Arrows,
- Connection in space,
- Numbers,
- Colours,
- Codes.

Put these together on a page, and what do you get? A Mind Map.

In transforming myself as a presenter, this was the only 'training' I gave myself, and it led to all the other attributes of being a good presenter. These days, my presentation skills get plenty of practice. In an average year, I give up to 120 presentations. The audiences could not be more different. I might be presenting to 1,000 educationally disadvantaged children or 7,000 university students in a football stadium, and I could be in any of a number of different countries around the world, from Australia to Mexico, Scotland to Singapore, addressing, perhaps, educational or governmental authorities. The presentations can vary hugely in length—anything from one hour to six weeks. In the business world, I present to organizations such as Oracle, HSBC, IBM, the Singapore Institute of Management, Barclays International, BP and Boeing, helping them plan major events or their long-term business strategy, or one-to-ones with company presidents or CEOs.

But whoever it is that I am addressing and whatever the subject, the preparation and planning has been exactly the same from the first day I first came to Mind Maps. Ever since then, the feedback I have received has been incredible. Audiences are asked to rank my presentations out of 100 and my average is 94.6. Saying this may seem immodest, but I am very proud of it. If I had to score myself as that young lecturer speaking about the power of my memory, I would give myself 20—and that would be for my desire to help the students and for my love of the subject. For my ability to convey that passion, I would give myself 0 because, if anything, I helped them to forget.

WHO, WHAT, WHY, WHEN, HOW?

If you take the time to Mind Map the basic facts of your presentation before you have even considered the specific topic of your talk, you will find it easier to focus on the right subject matter. You need to be clear about:

- Who your audience is;
- What they stand to benefit from listening to you.

Draw a Mind Map with your audience at the heart of it and imagine their expectations of your presentation. The branches off it represent those expectations. On a practical level, this could include:

- Illustrations,
- Facts,

- Case studies,
- Analysis.

On a broader level, your audience is looking to you for:

- Inspiration,
- Understanding,
- Insight,
- Relevance.

With the aid of this Mind Map, you can weave the practical content into a coherent order, ensuring that you have hard data to back up the insightful and inspirational points that you are making.

If you are speaking at a conference, workshop or symposium, it pays to find out who else is speaking and what they are planning to talk about. After examining the programme, Mind Map the other topics that are being touched on as part of your preparation. This will help you to avoid overlap, as well as give you a broader idea of how you fit into the overall proceedings.

YOUR PRESENTATION MIND MAP

Imagine you have been asked to give a presentation on how to market your online business at a conference where the theme for the day is: taking your business online.

1. Your first step is to Mind Map the conference so that your speech is relevant. If your presentation is about 'online business', ensure your central image encompasses the subject, so you might decide to draw a computer monitor with a pound or dollar sign on the screen.

2. Your main branches will include the subjects for discussion at the conference:

- the technical know-how necessary to take a business online;
- delivery systems for an online product or service;
- how to manage the customer service of an online operation.

Using information in the programme, draw sub-branches from each of the curved branches. One of these branches will denote your speech on marketing your online business.

3. Now concentrate on the sub-branches relating to your speech. These will include online marketing and offline marketing; within each of those sub-branches will be more specific ways of informing people about your online business, such as through e-mail marketing or direct mail.

If you approach a subject in this way, you will find it easier to stick to your subject. Your role in a wider context will be clearer and your thoughts and ideas are less likely to wander off on a tangent.

It pays to do your research as soon as you receive an invitation to make a presentation. And if you hear about a conference where it would be beneficial for you to speak, find out who is organizing it and ring them up to offer your services. This proactive approach is a godsend to conference organizers. Mind Map your area of expertise and how you could apply this to conferences throughout the calendar year. This puts you in a good position to prioritize the ones where it makes smart business sense for you to be seen and heard. The results could pay dividends for your company in the long term.

PRESENTATION CASE STUDY: BETA ROMEO DIAMOND

Imagine you work for a car company, Beta Romeo, which is trying to entice more male consumers to buying your latest small car, the Diamond. You are giving a presentation to a company which has expressed an interest in buying some of your cars to stock up their company car fleet, which are used mostly by male sales representatives.

You are presenting to them the results of research Beta Romeo commissioned about 'men and how their spending habits have changed over the last 10 years when it comes to what car to buy'. It transpires that men now have different priorities:

- Many of them may be fathers and so need a practical car which is big enough to accommodate their children;

- Men are more aware of environmental issues than they were 10 years ago and do not want a gas-guzzler.

You sit down to Mind Map your presentation and decide that your key message is 'small is beautiful', so this is at the heart of your Mind Map. (*See* colour Mind Map of the Beta Romeo Diamond Mind Map.)

Since your potential driver is likely to be a man, 'men' becomes one of the main branches of your Mind Map. This gives you an opportunity to reel off what the research revealed in greater depth, so you can talk about how men have changed and how much more progressive they have become when it comes to choosing a car. They no longer follow the philosophy of 'the bigger the better' when it comes to buying cars. Instead, their concerns are family and ethically oriented.

Use pictures on your Mind Map as a memory trigger for this. You want to change the traditional image of the company car as an unnecessarily big vehicle and make it something more user, family and environmentally friendly, so your Mind Map should emphasize this while emphasizing the negative aspects of large cars such as their expense, their impracticality and lack of versatility.

The other branches on your Mind Map branching from main headings such as 'image' and 'environment' can fill in the details, such as how having a smaller car benefits the environment, and reflects the moral and ethical concerns of today's progressive man.

PRACTICE

One of the branches on your Mind Map should focus on the practice you feel is necessary on your presentation to ensure that you do not overrun your allotted time, and to run through the presentation so that you are sure that you are the master of all the details. You can also use your Mind Map to help allocate how much time you want to spend on each topic, so you don't concentrate on one to the detriment of a another. Also, you can add some mental reminders to yourself about how you want the presentation to come over, such as 'strong', 'confident' and 'authoritative'.

PROPS

Of the presentations you have sat through in your life, how many do you remember? And how many just blur into a mass of PowerPoint slides, facts and figures, and uninspiring sales-speak? Now think about the presentations that you can remember. What made them so memorable?

It is likely there was a particular image that you can remember. If you want to share information with a group of people and get your point across, it helps to use images. Your audience will enjoy the distraction that they provide, they will stop them falling asleep, and it will make them more interested in *you*. To this end, when you are working on your presentation Mind Map, include a branch labelled 'props' so that you make it more fun, interactive and memorable for your audience.

When drawing the 'props' branch of the Beta Romeo Diamond Mind Map, remember that your theme is 'small is beautiful', so play up the fact that the car is small. Use your Mind Map to help focus on items that are small and beautiful. You could show a picture of a cute baby or a shining diamond. This way you are giving your presentation confidently, not defensively.

Remember to include a picture of the car, or preferably a few pictures which show off its exterior and interior. You are the link to the Beta Romeo Diamond, so make the most of being that link. Include swatches of the material that decorates the seats on your Mind Map that you can pass around so your audience gets a genuine feel for the car. Better still, include a Beta Romeo Diamond itself as one of your props, so you have a reminder on your Mind Map to arrange for cars to be available for your audience to test drive immediately after the presentation. By doing so you will be giving them a valuable experience which relates back to your entire presentation while information is still fresh in their minds.

This multi-sensory experience, coupled with the dynamic evidence that you have presented, will play a vital role in keeping the Beta Romeo Diamond front of mind when they are deciding which company car to use in their fleet.

COMPUTER MIND MAPS

In the age of PowerPoint many people expect state-of-the-art computer visuals during presentations. Computer Mind Maps—or indeed any Mind Map—can save your audiences from what the *International Herald Tribune* described as 'Death by PowerPoint'. Many presenters commit the fatal error of believing that to use PowerPoint effectively means simply listing a number of key words or phrases.

In reality, the pure brain-friendly term 'Power Point' means an integrated network of key ideas and images. Therefore, almost by definition, Mind Maps are *the* Power Point presentation tool, and they will keep audiences alert, learning and engaged. Mind Map programmes such as 'Mind Genius' can help you construct electronic Mind Maps to rival the most imaginative of Power-Point presentations.

Start by constructing a Master Mind Map (your Universal View) of the subject area. Each of the basic ordering ideas (main branches) will automatically manage themselves into the main chapter headings of your presentation. In turn, each of these can have a more detailed Mind Map constructed around it.

In many instances, you will find that the main branches of this 'chapter Mind Map' will also require a more detailed examination, necessitating a more magnified look at the details.

This process can continue until you have reached your appropriate level of magnification. The computer Mind Map software allows you to do this to 30 levels. The real-life work-application record so far, by the utility company Con Edison (*see* pp. 30–1), is 17 levels.

TRAINING PRESENTATIONS

If you are involved in training teams of people, Mind Maps are an ideal presentation tool. The three main methods of using Mind Maps in training presentations that I find most useful are:

1. COMPLETE MIND MAP

Prepare the full Mind Map of your lecture and present it to the course participants. When you discuss the Mind Map, start by highlighting the central image and outlining the main branches to give your audience an overview. Once you have done this, you can go on to investigate and explain your Mind Map in more detail. This method is especially useful for Mind Map-literate audiences who will immediately (and enthusiastically) recognize that you are a state-of-the-art presenter.

2. THE BUILD-UP

Another method is to build up the Mind Map as you share information with your audience. Once again, start with the central image and then add the main branches, briefly introducing what they mean. As you build the Mind Map, encourage your course participants to take notes in the form of their own individual versions of the Mind Map. This method is particularly useful for beginners, and it has the general advantage of helping the participants weave the meaning of the presentation into their own Mind Maps. Getting your audience to draw their own Mind Maps also requires your audience to think for themselves. Your course participants will get the most out of your presentations if you encourage active participation.

3. COLOUR/FILL-IN

The third method is to use a completed Mind Map, but not in colour. As you present your lecture you can get the participants to colour the key images, words and branches. Once again, this has the advantage of involving the students in a learning activity and gives them ownership of the Mind Map.

Noteworthy note-taking

For any presentation you give you should encourage your audience to use Mind Maps to take notes. Mind Maps allow participants to break the linear tyranny of traditional note-taking, and to build up the subject matter in a way which works with the brain's own natural logic. Taking notes with Mind Maps:

- Immediately engages the brains of your audience and encourages radiant thinking;
- Helps your audience make appropriate associations and absorb information more effectively;
- Encourages active participation and retains audience interest.

PRESENTATIONS FOR BUSINESS STUDIES

Nowadays, more and more workers are studying for vocational qualifications, either by combining work with part-time study or by engaging in a full-time course at the beginning of their career. Presentations are increasingly used on such courses as a means of bringing the students' minds into focus, and as a spark for ideas for discussion between groups of students and between individual students and their lecturers.

Using Mind Maps can help make the ideas flow more freely. Dividing up different aspects of business into the branches of a Mind Map can assist in simplifying daunting aspects of business into a visually comprehensible and much more manageable plan of action.

So many presentations now entail sophisticated technology that a presentation without it is becoming a rare event in the business world. A Mind Map will help you stay in control of the numerous and diverse threads of your dynamic presentation, including the props, without recourse to such technology.

If you have a Mind Map to hand of everything you want to say, you will remember it more clearly and it will be easier for you to stay on message with your thoughts and ideas. And you won't have the added worry of dealing with any technology which can play havoc with your nerves.

Using Mind Maps for study

Lance Brown is one such student who understands the benefits of how Mind Maps can be applied in this way.

'I am a student studying at London Metropolitan University in Moorgate. I am creating a Mind Map for one of my units—Design for Business Managers. We are asked to create a product or service and learn how we are going to produce it and market it. We have to understand what concepts we need to engage and involve people. I have used a Mind Map to understand all the concepts and to create a visual look at all aspects. My aspects include marketing,

---

> *location and financial, as well as understanding where my target market is going to be. Sometimes I use small pictures instead of words to make it look attractive and so that my lecturer can see straight away without needing me to explain. He sees different aspects and the project is actually expanding in his own mind while I am explaining it to him. It is a great way of getting the idea across very quickly. Every time I go back to it I think I could expand the idea a little more.'*

Follow-up questions

When your presentation is over, you will have stimulated interest among your audience and a number of them will have questions to ask you. This is great experience; whatever form of presentations you give in your business life, question and answer sessions are always golden opportunities to capitalize on the interest you have stimulated, making sure that any doubts or queries are settled in a positive fashion.

When you were at school and had an exam coming up, you might have wondered: 'If I was the person setting this test, what kind of questions would I ask that would most effectively draw out the students' knowledge?' The same principle applies in business. If you know there is going to be a question and answer session after your presentation, then use a Mind Map to be prepared for it.

Draw a questions Mind Map in advance of your presentation, with each branch representing one area that you think you will be asked about. That way, you can work out your answers and take them with you to the presentation. Your audience will be impressed at your ability to remember relevant facts and figures in a spontaneous fashion.

If there are any questions asked which you haven't covered in the Mind Map, be sure to make a note of them so that you can incorporate them into future Mind Maps and improve your performance even further in the future.

TAKING THE MONOTONY OUT OF MEETINGS

Now you now know how to deliver the optimum presentation using Mind Maps, you can apply a similar set of tactics to help take the monotony out of meetings.

In *board*rooms across the globe, people are sat in meetings, *bored*. They have long given up paying attention and their minds are wandering a million miles from the room and the subject matter. Just as they are thinking about their next holiday, or what they are going to have for dinner that night, suddenly all eyes turn to them as they hear the dreaded words: 'So, what do you think?'

Jolted back into the real word, fragments and odd words that may have drifted into their brains from the meeting now take on massive significance. In the end, they decide to play safe, mumbling something along the lines of: 'I think I'd need more information before committing myself either way' or 'I think that needs a bit more research'. Solid, catch-all phrases in the average boardroom that can be used to dig yourself out of any large hole into which you've toppled by losing concentration.

No boredrooms at Boeing

Sam Brooks and Dan O'Connell are design engineers at Boeing. In meetings, Sam regularly uses Mind Maps to control the discussion and establish a sense of order. He says:

> *'I have to have order or it just doesn't work for me. And the Mind Map is one of the tools that I use. When it comes to defining or creating something, Mind Maps give me a head start.*
>
> *'We have a lot of strong, smart people here. They all have their own ideas which can tend to get out of control. One of the best ways to get hold of those ideas and keep their attention is to go up to the board. I draw a cloud and in that cloud I'll put a word. And I'll turn around to the gang and say, "OK, who wants to put something up here?" and I'll put a word up and another word and the first thing you know is the guys have settled down. They're working together because somebody has stopped it from being crazy.'*

If you use Mind Maps to help run meetings, you will avoid people's brains deciding to take a spontaneous holiday.

GOLDEN RULES FOR PRODUCTIVE MEETINGS

1. Keep to the agenda on the Mind Map. If you have five topics that need discussing, then make sure *all five* topics get discussed within the time available. On your Mind Map you will have indicated how much time can afford to be spent on each topic. This will prevent you coming to the second topic and then realizing that you have only five minutes left.

2. Keep the content relevant. If someone is threatening to go off on a tangent that is neither interesting nor appropriate, bring them back to the discussion in hand, or move on to your next point on the Mind Map.

189

3. Make sure everyone is aware of the agenda as outlined by the Mind Map so that they come prepared. It is disruptive and counterproductive to have people dashing in and out of the room to fetch material they have forgotten. The only interruptions should be for breaks in a long meeting. (No meeting should go on for longer than an hour without a short comfort break—longer than this and the brains around the table will be flagging.)

4. If it is a regular meeting, remember to have the Mind Maps from the last meeting to hand. It will provide a structure, helping to ensure that you don't miss anything, as well as providing an opportunity to review and update them.

5. Too many cooks spoil the broth—if there are people in your meeting who don't really need to be there, then make sure their time isn't being wasted when they could be doing something more productive. Don't just exclude them, but explain to them by showing them on the Mind Map why they don't fit into that particular scenario, otherwise they might feel hurt or rejected.

Mind Mapping can transform those meetings that used to bore you, as well as those presentations that used to fill you with panic. Mind Maps help you stay in control of your agenda, making business more dynamic than ever. Here are the crucial points to keep in mind:

- Plan your presentations using Mind Maps so that you are relevant, interesting and, above all, memorable.
- Make your presentation multi-sensory so that your audience remembers you and what you had to say.
- Use Mind Maps throughout meetings to help you stick to your agenda.
- Extend the use of Mind Maps as a colourful and effective way of filing 'minutes'.

Clearly, Mind Maps are perfect for structuring and organizing current ideas and plans in a memorable way for presenting to others. They are also the prime tool for structuring and checking areas of your life outside the work-place. In our final chapter, we will look at how Mind Maps can help you achieve and maintain the all-important 'work–life balance'.

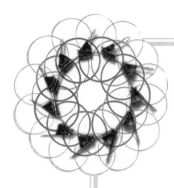

8

Work–Life
Balance
Solutions

The demands of juggling a career with family life and other outside commitments and interests can be immense. So it is particularly important that you feel comfortable with the balance you strike, and that you do not over-compromise on any area of your life that is important to you. As the subtitle of this book, 'How to be the best at your job and still have time to play', suggests, those of you already using Mind Maps at work will already be well on the way to achieving a good work–life balance.

By following the advice in the preceding chapters, you should be able to find the time to do all the things you really want or need to do, as well as leaving yourself space to deal with anything unforeseen that might crop up. Mind Maps are the prime tool for this, bringing organization and clarity to your life, and they are every bit as useful for your life outside work.

This work–life balance is a dynamic process that needs constant attention and fine-tuning. When Mind Mapping such a holistic view of your life, you will need to incorporate all the important elements of your life beyond your work, including your health, diet, rest and relaxation, as well as making arrangements to see your extended family and friends. In addition, it is in the interests of an employer or team leader to be aware that it is in the interests of the team and individuals alike that an equitable balance is maintained.

Here is one person's experience of using Mind Maps to balance work and home life.

> **Balancing family life with work**
>
> Rosalind Gower is a working mother and a television producer at the BBC. She says:
>
> *'Mind Maps have changed my whole life. As a working mother, you are always being torn in loads of different directions, so if I set up a home Mind Map with 'work' branches and 'kids' branches and all the other responsibilities that working mothers have, I don't forget anything. If you say to yourself, "I must book a dental appointment", you just stick it in the relevant branch of the Mind Map.*
>
> *'And at work, when I start any new project, I have a whole variety of information and so it's important to try and categorize that and get people working on different aspects. I use a Mind Map and that is really effective: everybody is responsible for one branch of the Mind Map and I am at the centre overseeing it all. It is very successful.'*

WORK–LIFE BALANCE: THE EMPLOYER'S POINT OF VIEW

Enlightened companies realize that the family is the major supporter of or detractor from a company's energy and goal accomplishment. To this end, they will invite family members—parents, children, spouses and siblings—to the company premises, where they will learn more about the company's goals and vision through the use of Mind Maps. In this way, they will not only become supporters of the work team, but also members of the extended team themselves.

A family affair

The Young Presidents' Organization is a network of 8,000 young global leaders from 75 different countries with its headquarters in Irving, Texas. One of their declared core values is that 'Family participation in YPO activities enhances the growth and development of all involved'.

To this end, all family members are invited to learn how to use Mind Maps, and through this medium, the functions of the organization are explained. In addition, a visit to the workplace allows them to gain visual details of what that team member does and accomplishes at YPO.

This initiative creates great team spirit and energy, and when a team member goes to work, they go with the love, support and best wishes of their family. And when, occasionally, they do need to work overtime, this is understood and accepted.

Maintaining a healthy work–life balance should be high on the agenda of employers. Keen to maintain the highest possible calibre of staff, employers are coming round to the idea of being more flexible in their attitudes.

A forward-thinking employer conducts regular staff surveys and Mind Maps the results. Main branches might include flexible working options such as '3–4-day weeks', 'job-sharing', 'home-working', 'provision of laptops, mobiles, broadband' and 'remote access to computer servers', with sub-branches looking at each in further detail.

If a particular option begins to look feasible, such as flexible working, then a separate Mind Map can probe the practicalities of implementing such a policy. For instance, the costs of the scheme can be mapped alongside the potential cost and human resource involved in having to replace members of staff who opt to move to a more flexible workplace.

Showing the company has a human face does not cost anything but can reap dividends. For instance, if the washing machine leaks all over the kitchen floor one morning, that is the kind of the thing that happens to everyone. Accepting these are just facts of life and understanding that they need to be dealt with is an enlightened approach that will be much appreciated in the workplace and will help build a more relaxed working environment.

If you are an employer wishing to improve the work–life balance of your staff, Mind Map the ways in which you can do so.

BRINGING BALANCE TO THE WORKPLACE

1. Draw a central image which sums up work–life balance: a literal interpretation could be a pair of scales with 'work' on one side and 'balance' on the other. As we saw earlier (*see* p. 109), if all areas of the business have been Mind Mapped thoroughly, and work equates to play, then any consideration of work–life balance should, in fact, be one of play–life balance. Your central image could reflect this.

2. The main branches will depend on the specific requirements and situation of your company. It is likely that two of them might be 'flexitime' and 'childcare'; 'working from home' could be another option if the work can largely be done on a computer. However, this is clearly not the case if your line of business involves face-to-face contact with customers.

3. Explore your options through sub-branches and cost them out. For instance, company crèches or contributions towards childcare are a very attractive benefit for employees, although costly to provide. However, this can be a worthwhile investment since the employer has an employee with peace of mind about their child's welfare.

4. If your company has recently undertaken a staff survey, incorporate their comments into your Mind Map. Use a different colour to mark out this input.

5. Discuss your Mind Map with your team at work, incorporating their feedback and comments, again in different colours.

It may be that you will not want to introduce too many innovations and changes into the workplace in one go. However, by listening to your staff and taking steps to smooth the potential frictions that can exist on the interface between work and home life you are providing the kind of work culture that is a magnet for talented and motivated team members.

It is a good idea to use your Mind Map as a blueprint for progress, keeping it updated as you make changes in the workplace.

PARTNERS AND TEAMWORK

You can imagine the scenario. It is a Friday evening and you are supposed to be meeting your partner for dinner. You are sitting at a restaurant table, surrounded by happy loving couples, laughing and looking lovingly into each other's eyes. You check your watch again—your partner is running an hour late.

Eventually, when your partner arrives, you have been sitting on your own in a restaurant for an hour, feeling lonely and humiliated. A covincing array of excuses does not help in the slightest. As far as you are concerned, your partner has made work a priority over you. Even if you are thoroughly supportive of your partner's work, there may still be occasions when you feel let down.

With the pressures involved with you both being busy people, how can you make sure that similar situations do not keep on recurring? The solution for both of you is to plan ahead by using Mind Maps and make it clear where the boundaries are. This can only be achieved by constant (and non-confrontational) communication.

Avoiding confrontation

As soon as a contentious issue emerges, the tendency can be to argue round in circles, the arguments going over the same old ground as both of you waste valuable time and energy without reaching a solution. And worse, all too often the argument can degenerate and spiral downwards into a meaningless and hurtful dispute.

Instead, it is an easy matter to plan your time ahead with Mind Maps. If, for instance, you argue regularly about your respective commitments for the coming week, by using Mind Maps it becomes a straightforward affair to see how your plans mesh together and if and where adjustments need to be made (*see* Chapter 3). If there is still an impasse, then together you could prioritize your commitments on the Mind Map or mark the ones which would be easiest to re-arrange.

If you both get in the habit of Mind Mapping your engagements and then sharing this with each other, these sorts of conflicts are less likely to occur.

Teamwork

You often hear it said of a couple who seem to get along together that they 'make a good team'. The rules of good teamwork apply just as much to personal relationships as they do to business, so all the advice in this book on helping a team to focus clearly on joint goals and priorities is relevant here (*see* Chapter 5, 'Leading Your Team to Success').

Mind Maps can be used when tackling any thorny issue to help encourage healthy debate and discussion. This can range from minor decisions, such as finding the best time to take off work for a short break or where to go on holiday, to major decisions about career changes which may even involve re-location. On p. 202 is an example of a Mind Map used to decide where to go on holiday. The family have all put on the Mind Map where they would like to go, and what they would like to do when they get there. After discussion, the information has been condensed into a branch of 'possibilities', with destinations in Thailand and New Zealand explored further. From this point it will be an easy matter to decide on a destination and set of activities which will please everyone.

By using Mind Maps to plan together, you are working productively and proactively as a team. If there are difficulties to be faced, then you can face them together, finding the best way forward in full knowledge of the facts. And you will be able to revisit your priorities regularly, and remind yourself what is important to you.

Using Mind Maps helps to stop work from seeping into your home life. Everyone needs breaks, no matter how dedicated they are. By Mind Mapping, you are helping each other to be more effective both in the relationship and at work.

Growing the team: children

If you have established a good way of being together as a couple, integrating your work lives into your relationship, there may come a point when you wonder how the pair of you would manage if there were new additions to your team, requiring even more of your love, empathy, tolerance and attention.

The decision to become parents is a massive milestone in any relationship, and one that can turn a hitherto smooth-running partnership upside-down. In addition, no matter how many books you read and classes you go to, the realities of parenthood remain a huge learning curve.

Children need your time, love, attention and energy more than anyone or anything else in your life. While some parents prefer to cope by themselves, or are not in a position to be able to employ regular help, others choose to employ additional help to help ease the burden. If this is the case, then Mind Map the childcare options open to you:

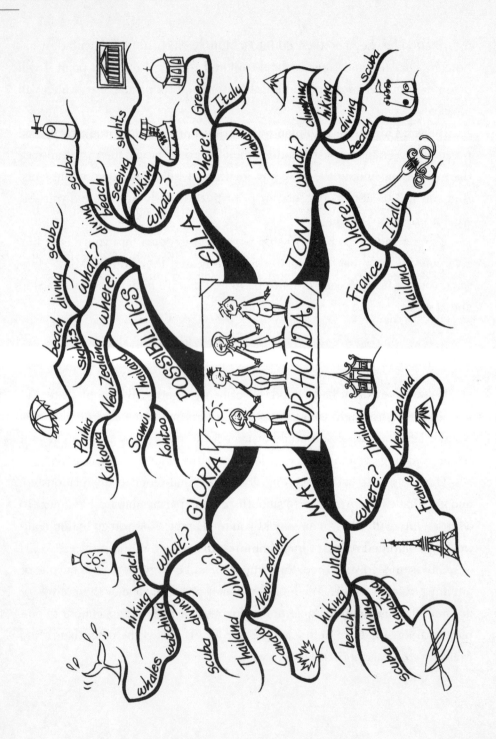

MIND MAPS FOR CHILDCARE

1. Use a photo or drawing of your child as your central image. Their happiness and well-being is your priority.

2. Draw curved branches from the central image to represent your options. These could include 'family', 'friends', 'nanny' and 'nursery'. Keep to one word per line.

3. Extend your thinking on each option by using sub-branches. For instance, you could have a nanny who comes to work at your house every day or who lives in. You could also use your sub-branches to explore if a nanny-share would work with one of your friends or neighbours. For friends, you could add to your Mind Map those who you think might help on a regular basis, perhaps as part of a reciprocal arrangement, whereby you can child-mind when you are not at work. Explore all the possible options open to you, taking into account when they are available and at what cost, to enable you to make a balanced decision.

STRESS FROM WORK

Stress can have severe repercussions on physical and mental health, and impact adversely on life at work and at home; as a consequence, relationships with friends and loved ones may become strained. Eliminating stress from work will help maintain a healthy home–work balance. Without this, all kinds of tensions and difficulties can build up.

Stress is not exclusive to management positions—it affects all kinds of workers in all kinds of workplaces. The physical signs of stress include:

- backache,
- skin complaints,
- excessive sweating,

- headaches or migraines,
- indigestion.

The behavioural signs include:

- insomnia,
- aggression,
- comfort-eating or loss of appetite,
- poor concentration.

The psychological signs include:

- mood swings,
- obsessive thoughts,
- low self-esteem and self-confidence,
- anger,
- anxiety.

Minimizing stress

Stress is a negative phenomenon which feeds on itself. It saps your health, energy and efficiency. And because when you are stressed you accomplish less, your stress increases in a vicious spiral, until you reach the point of collapse.

Mind Maps are the ideal stabilizer when you find yourself in a stressful situation, stemming the tide of negative thoughts and events. If you Mind Map everything that is causing you stress, you will be able to sort through to identify the real causes. Then you will be able to Mind Map a plan of action (*see* Chapter 3 for how to Mind Map solutions to short-term problems, as well as planning for the long term to ensure problems do not recur) so you are able to move forward in your life.

If you prioritize your plans, starting with the root causes of your stress first, as you work through your plan of action you will be able to cross out the causes of your stress on your Mind Map, one by one. This will be akin to a visual representation of the stress dropping away from you, and the act of doing so will contribute to a growing positive frame of mind.

And, by getting into the habit of Mind Mapping and planning ahead, you will remain confident that you have your affairs in hand, leaving your mind unclouded by stress and your imagination free to roam.

Exercising for life

Exercise is a wonderful tool for de-stressing your life. And keeping fit enables you to work most efficiently and creatively, as well as getting the most out of your home life. All too often, however, good intentions can get lost in your struggle to balance your work–home life.

My own exercise regime is a routine in which I stay aerobically fit, muscularly fit and flexible. When I am at home, I row on the river 6–7 am. I take a minimum of two walks a week of up to an hour and a half in local parks or countryside. I also do yoga and martial arts stretching and exercises. When I am travelling, I make sure that I have access to a swimming pool where I do at least half an hour in a pool, and a gym where I do a full machine and weights work-out, combined with stretching. And, most importantly, every now and again I take two days off when I do absolutely nothing.

But I am very much in the minority. In the UK, a shocking 70% of the population take no regular exercise, which is a worrying statistic when you consider that the average Briton will spend, on average, 14 years of their life sitting down.

In the light of this, it is vital that you make exercise part of your weekly routine and avoid the lure of the comfy sofa at the end of a long day at work.

HAVE FUN WITH FITNESS

Exercise should be fun, so start by preparing a fitness Mind Map:

1. Draw a picture of yourself in the middle, super-fit and primed for action.

2. Your main branches can include all the main forms of exercise that you enjoy. It can be anything from salsa dancing to snow-boarding, tai-chi to team sports. If you have ever been curious about a certain form of exercise, then include it in your Mind Map.

3. Add sub-branches to include more details about each form of exercise. For example, discover if there is a salsa class near you at home or at work and find out if you need any particular clothing. Include the details on your Mind Map.

4. Show your Mind Map to your friends and see if anyone is interested in joining you in your chosen activities. Depending on the sort of person you are, it may be that the more of you there are, the more motivated you will be and the more likely you are to stick to it.

5. Chart your exercise progress on your Mind Map and keep the chart in a place where you can see it. If you notice yourself losing weight or gaining in energy having got into the routine of regular exercise, then write it on the Mind Map as this may be a motivation for you to keep going.

As well as planning regular exercise activities, you should give thought to how much exercise you benefit from as you go about your everyday activities. In particular, do you resort to using the car or public transport to work when you could just as easily walk or cycle.

TWO FEET OR FOUR WHEELS

Driving has become our preferred method of transport, but you can stop yourself from becoming car dependent, improving your aerobic fitness by walking or cycling instead of automatically reaching for your car keys.

Draw a Mind Map to see if there are any situations where you could walk or cycle instead of driving:

1.   Draw a pair of walking boots or a bicycle as your central image.

2.   Using one word along your main branches, summarize the journeys you make every week with your car. You might include 'work', 'school run', 'friends', 'shops', 'gym' or 'family'.

3.   Expand on your main branches with sub-branches and investigate alternatives. Perhaps there is a scenic route you could cycle to work, instead of driving. Maybe you could walk the children to school instead of taking them in the car and that way they would get some exercise too.

4.   Just as with the fitness Mind Map above, keep this Mind Map close to hand, on a noticeboard or on your fridge door so you can keep a check on how much walking you are doing, noting the fitness benefits as you go.

Walking is also wonderful for clearing the mind and offering perspective on a situation, as we saw with the Roman problem-solving technique, *solvitas perambulum* (*see* p. 33–4).

Conversely, sitting in a car in a traffic jam, unable to move and breathing in traffic fumes is a sure-fire way to increase your stress levels.

WORKING FROM HOME

Having done all your research and made a business plan (*see* Chapter 3, pp. 47–8), you have decided to go it alone. You have converted your spare room into an office and bought a workstation, computer, printer, phone and office chair. You have installed broadband and e-mail—and you have a beautiful view of the garden which you hope will inspire creative ideas. The light is good and places no strain on your eyes, and the room is away from the road so there is no noise.

Dealing with distractions

On your first morning, you make yourself a hot drink and settle down to work. After a few minutes, your eye is caught by the mass of weeds that seem to have sprung up out of nowhere in your garden. With a gasp, you leap to your feet, rush down into the garden and pull them up. Then you notice a shrub that is looking a bit untidy and give it a good trim. By the time you get back to your desk, your drink is cold, so you go to the kitchen to make yourself another. Then you notice the breakfast things still haven't been washed up and . . . You get the picture.

We all like the idea of working from home, but not everyone finds it easy to keep to a disciplined routine and ignore the potential distractions.

At work, the sole purpose of being there is to work. The home, by contrast, has many different functions. It is a sanctuary for relaxation, a place where you entertain friends and family, and a home where you tuck your children into bed at night.

Some distractions are unavoidable. For instance, when the phone rings, you may not know if it is a business call or someone ringing up for a chat; in the same way, if the doorbell rings, you are unlikely to resist going to the door. But many distractions *can* be controlled.

Distractions are where your mind is constantly drawn to other visions.

This is because we are always aware of the whereabouts of pleasing things. If your work is ill-defined or undirected, your brain will unfocus, spending time on all the 'good' stuff and avoiding the pain.

Mind Maps are a self-motivating device. As soon as you Mind Map your month/week/day ahead, you will refocus on the tasks in hand. Checking off the branches as you accomplish them will give you a feeling of achievement. If there are items on your Mind Map which you are looking forward to, then you can view these as rewards. Your brain will know that you can have them only when you actually deserve them.

Finding a routine

It is important to order your day and punctuate it with regular breaks. As well as keeping your brain fresh, this will give the day some shape and structure. It will not help your business if you find yourself enjoying a lie-in until midday and then having to work all night when your partner comes home.

Also, you do need to be able to enjoy some of the benefits that the flexibility of working from home offers you. When you are making your week-ahead Mind Map, you will be able to factor in occasional times when you are able to take an afternoon off and do something outside—go shopping on a Wednesday instead of a Saturday, or enjoy a walk in the park on a sunny day.

Tips for working from home successfully

1. Work from home if you can make enough money. In the US, only 70% of home businesses earn the same as their full-time office-based equals. Are you happy to take a pay cut if you need to, and can you afford this? As well as a business plan Mind Map including realistic financial aims, ensure that

---

you have Mind Mapped any other goals that might be included in your reason to work from home (e.g. you may be studying part-time, or looking after children).

2. Customize your own space. Mind Map how you are going to decorate your office and don't forget to include important extras such as professional certificates, photos of friends and family and books which you think might be helpful. These things will help to inspire you when you need it most and make your office a better creative environment.

3. If you have a partner or children, make sure that they know when it is OK to come and disturb you—and when it is not. There might be certain times when you need to work flat out to meet a deadline and other times when you can be more flexible. So they don't worry about getting their head bitten off *every* time they appear in your office doorway, pin up a week-ahead Mind Map to indicate when your office is out of bounds.

4. Create a support network. There are likely to be other people in the area who are in the same situation. If so, they can come to be an equivalent of workplace colleagues. Combating loneliness, particularly after the lively atmosphere of some offices, can be difficult for home-workers. Make new friends and meet up every so often; you can swap ideas and benefit from the support of people going through the same experience as you.

It is helpful to get out regularly, otherwise the liberating benefits of working from home can be lost and you might begin to resent feeling trapped in your own home. Exercising your flexibility in this way will emphasize the benefits of your new life, putting you in control of your time and how you choose to spend it.

OPTIMUM PERFORMANCE

Finding an equilibrium in your life between the demands of work and the commitments of your personal life is not always easy. It may be you are:

- Trying to stop your work life intruding too much into your home life;
- Working from home and attempting to keep distractions at bay;
- Needing to organize and fine-tune your work–life balance to avoid any conflicts of interest.

However, your ultimate goal should be to enjoy and welcome *all* areas of your life. While work may be a necessity, it should *and can* remain a pleasure. We are all different, and while some find satisfaction in total dedication and absorption in one single area, for others the joy lies in embracing all the stimulating experiences life has to offer.

In any case, whether you are self-employed or a CEO, Mind Maps are the prime tool for achieving this harmony, allowing you to enjoy and give optimum performance and achieve total satisfaction in your life.

INDEX

Buzan Centres

Email: Buzan@BuzanCentres.com
Website: www.Mind-Map.com

Or:

Buzan Centres Ltd. (Rest of World)
54 Parkstone Road
Poole
Dorset
BH15 2PG
United Kingdom

Tel: +44 1202 674676
Fax: +44 1202 674776

Buzan Centres Inc. (Americas)
PO Box 4
Palm Beach, FL 33480

Tel: 561-881-0188
Fax: 561-434-1682

Make the most of your mind today

ALSO BY TONY BUZAN

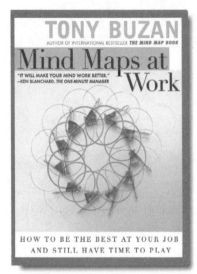

ISBN 0-452-28682-4
Price $18.00

ISBN 0-452-27322-6
Price $25.00

ISBN 0-452-26604-1
Price $13.00

ISBN 0-452-26603-3
Price $14.00

Plume
A Member of Penguin Group (USA) Inc.
www.penguin.com

Available wherever books are sold.